Killers
OF THE
Dream

Books by Lillian Smith

STRANGE FRUIT

KILLERS OF THE DREAM

NOW IS THE TIME

ONE HOUR

MEMORY OF A LARGE CHRISTMAS

OUR FACES, OUR WORDS

THE JOURNEY

THE WINNER NAMES THE AGE

LILLIAN SMITH

Killers
OF THE
Dream

Revised and Enlarged

W · W · NORTON & COMPANY

New York · London

Norton Library edition first published 1978.

A portion of Chapter I, Part One, in somewhat different form, appeared in and was copyrighted by *Common Ground* in 1943. Chapter 2, Part Three, also in somewhat different form, was published in *South Today*, copyright 1943, by Lillian E. Smith.

Books That Live
The Norton imprint on a book means that in the publisher's estimation
it is a book not for a single season but for the years.
W. W. Norton & Company, Inc.

The Library of Congress Catalogued the First Edition

E185 as follows:
61 Smith, Lillian Eugenia, 1897–1966
S64 Killers of the dream. Rev. and enl. New York, Norton [1961]
1961 253 p. 22 cm.

1. Negroes—Southern States. 2. Southern States—Soc. condit.
I. Title.
E185.61.S64 1961 917.5 61–8781‡
Library of Congress [10]

W. W. Norton & Company, Inc., 500 Fifth Avenue, New York, NY 10110
W. W. Norton & Company Ltd, 10 Coptic Street, London WC1A 1PU

ISBN 0-393-00884-3

PRINTED IN THE UNITED STATES OF AMERICA

5 6 7 8 9 0

Contents

PART THREE
Giants in the Earth

PART FOUR
The Dream and Its Killers

Killers

OF THE

Dream

Foreword:
A letter to my publisher

Dear George:

I have just now finished reading *Killers of the Dream*. And am here on the mountain thinking about it.

Or am I <u>dreaming</u>? For pieces of a small Deep South town are floating past me; the wonder, the absurdities of faraway years skim by like blowing mirrors. And tangled with it are swamps and lakes and the river that used to disappear overnight, leaving white sand and pools of gasping fish—and beyond, back of everything, moss and oaks and cypress: they slide close, refusing their role as background, and seem now to be forces pressing me into conformity with primordial patterns.

Perhaps, long ago, they did just that; perhaps they, too, bent our imaginations to their shape and whispered their orders to our moral natures as insistently as did the invisible walls and chasms "real people" made which blocked southern children in so many directions.

The book brings it back: the ruthless games . . . the protectiveness of those who loved us . . . the smells—how stubbornly they cling to everything! Raw smells: of barnyard and privy, of dishwater and hog-killing, and turpentine stills, of sweat glands defending the body against fear. But there were gentler smells, too: yellow jessamine and wild bays, and wet green pecans and warm coconut pie and hot iron against clean linen, and waxed rosewood; and dried petals in the blue bowl in the parlor. Demanding of the memory, these smells, as they pull you from room to room of that endless house you were born in, dragging you to kitchen to backyard to woodhouse to smokehouse to stables, to the lilies in your mother's garden, up the stairs to the library where you cloistered yourself from questions you could not help asking but found no answers to: Who is God? what is eternity? why is death? where are heaven and hell? where did I come from? and where am I going? when is the end of time? and where is the end of space? and who am I? besides a name, what else? and who is this other Self that watches me? does it go to sleep when I do?

And there were the other questions—much closer to everyday life: the brutal ones.

—And the edgy blackness and whiteness of things . . . the breathing symbols we made of the blackness and the whiteness . . . the metaphors we created and watched ourselves turning into . . . the shaky myths we leaned on even as we changed them into weapons to defend us against external events.

Now, suddenly, shoving out pleasures and games and stinging questions come the TERRORS: the Ku Klux Klan and the lynchings I did not see but recreated from whispers of grownups . . . the gentle back-door cruelties of "nice people" which scared me more than the cross burnings . . . and the singsong voices of politicians who preached their demonic suggestions to us as if elected by Satan to do so: telling us lies about skin color and a culture they were callously ignorant of—lies made of their own fantasies, of their secret deviations—forcing decayed pieces of theirs and the region's obscenities into the minds of the young and leaving them there to fester.

Listening, I'd see my little colored friends on the rim of the crowd, silent and big-eyed and vaguely smiling, not knowing what else to do; or maybe the Negro doctor who moved with dignity and spoke with quietness might be standing there; or far back, a few of the colored mill-hands—and a slow horror would drain the blood from my throat and I would think, He is saying these things not caring that they hear, as if they were not human! And then would come the tearing dialogue: *Well, are they? are they? of course they are! they're just like me! but are you sure? Of course! then why are they not in our church? why are they not in our school? why can't we keep playing together? what is wrong what is wrong—*

I am afraid this book has played tricks on me: I am caught again in those revolving doors of childhood.

It is a book brought to life, I see plainly now, by young questions that begged for sane answers, by un-verbalized fears that claimed a right to be encapsuled in words, by a need to bridge fissures, to tie belief and fact and dream and act closer together.

But I wrote it for another reason: I wrote it because I had to find out what life in a segregated culture had done to me, one person; I had to put down on paper these experiences so that I could see their meaning for me. I was in dialogue with myself as I wrote, as well as with my hometown and my childhood and history and the future, and the past. Writing is both horizontal and vertical exploration. It has to true itself with facts but also with feelings and symbols, and memories that are never quite facts but sometimes closer to the "truth" than is any fact.

You have said that only a southerner could have written this book: only one who feels deep in the bone the cruel perplexities and paradoxes of our way of life. And it is true: I have written "as a southerner," but I have written as one who also feels at home throughout the world. Perhaps more truly, I have written simply as a person.

[Coming back to the book after these years, I opened it wondering if what I was about to read would seem authentic to me. For I have changed since writing it. I am different. Because I wrote it. In the writing I explored layers of my nature which I had never touched before; in reliving my distant small childhood my imagination stretched and enclosed my whole life; my beliefs changed as I wrote them down. As is true of any writing that comes out of one's own existence, the experiences themselves were transformed during the act of writing by awareness of new meanings which settled down on them.] There happened to me this thing that Erich Kahler speaks of: "All utterance," he said, ". . . be it 'language' or shaping of objects, tends to expand and eventually to split the being from which it comes." He was writing of the nature of the symbol and said in the same essay, "The symbol originates in the split of existence, the confrontation and communication of an inner with an outer reality, whereby a meaning detaches itself from sheer existence." I like that. But I see it, too, another way:[the writer transcends her material in the act of looking at it, and since part of that material is herself, a metamorphosis takes place: *something happens within:* a new chaos, and then slowly, a new being.]

And I am sure the years which followed the writing of this book—filled as they were with the writing of more books, and with travel and study, and with a few ordeals which seemed inescapable—brought their mutations, also.

It pleases me, therefore, to find validity and poignancy as I read it now. Its inner drama seems exciting and firmly motivated. The facts, twelve years after they were written down, are still accurate. Obscure areas of the human experience are illuminated more surely than I had thought. And its relevance for this hour we are living in astonishes me. For what was based on intuition, on a kind of prophetic guess, is now boldly acting itself out on a world-size stage. I had felt the curve of approaching events but I could only warn, I could not prove. And now here it is: the new African nations, the hatred of colonialism, and the Communists' shrewd exploitation of this word so fatefully tied to "the white man" and to Western democracy—and to everyone's future.

When I wrote those chapters I was afraid—I am more afraid, today—that we may not break our bondage to past errors in time to win the confidence of young nations who need our help. And whom we desperately need. I watched with a sense of horror—I am still watching—the hands of the Southern clock (and the American clock) move with death-slowness while the world clock speeds along as if stuffed with the energy of a rocket.

And now, there is Cuba. Ninety miles away, a Communist government. How could it have happened! Why are we so blind to each disaster as it begins slowly, slowly, and then rushes toward us! Is it complacency? But what causes this kind of complacency, so unreal, so without substance? Why are we suppressing anxiety, denying danger? Why apathy—when we desperately need moral energy? why flabby spirits when we need iron strength?

Colonialism was once a harsh exploitation of peoples; today, it is a symbol stalking the earth. And men live and die by their symbols. To Asia and Africa—and Cuba, yes —the word means shame and degradation, it means dehumanization, poverty, pain. And here, in this great country whose people love freedom and respect men as human beings, colonialism's twin brother, segregation, not only lives but wields power, and earth-shaking decisions are made by its followers. But the new nations of Asia and Africa are making earth-shaking decisions, too; they have it within their power to do so not only in the United Nations, not only in secret sessions with Russia and China, but in the secret rooms of the people's memory.

Why can we not see the pattern laid out so plainly before our eyes? Ghana . . . Mali . . . Guinea . . . Tanganyika . . . Kenya . . . Liberia . . . Nigeria . . . Mauritania . . . Republic of Chad . . . Republic of Niger . . . Angola . . . Southwest Africa . . . Nyasaland . . . Southern Rhodesia . . . Northern Rhodesia . . . Mozambique . . . Sudan . . . Somalia . . . Central African Republic . . . the Congo . . . Bechuanaland . . . South Africa . . . Malagasy . . . Basutoland . . . Swaziland . . . Gabon . . . Republic of Ivory Coast . . . Senegal . . . Ethiopia . . . and others and others. Mixed together, as I have jumbled them here, the free and the not yet free, they are Africa below the Desert, Africa in struggle with itself, Africa smeared by old bleeding memories, reaching out for a future called "Africa for the Africans" which may turn into mirage because of a too urgent hunger to be and to become. Too urgent? Yes. For starvation can be exploited by unscrupulous leaders; it is easier to arouse hatred of others than love for one's own freedom and future; it is easy, too, for these leaders in their difficulties to appeal to color just as southern demagogues did when the South was in chaos after the Civil War. We should not be surprised if we hear in African accents words about Black Supremacy, just as we still hear in southern accents words about White Supremacy. The fine concept of the human being may get lost in the shuffle and we may face a black racism just as white racism is disappearing. This is possible although it would be tragic error.

But whatever wisdom or irresponsible ambition their leaders may show, these new nations need us: our financial and technical aid, our moral support, our acceptance of their citizens as human beings.

But we cannot give them support or acceptance, no matter how eloquently we may offer it, until we rid our own country of racism and its primitive rites of segregation. The President may try, the State Department, the USIA and Peace Corps may try, but no matter what they do or say, the offer of help and friendship will be without psychic and moral substance as long as we practice segregation here at home. And at the critical moment, many of these nations, too, will turn to communism, rejecting what they call "white democracy."

Our President and his executive office can achieve much; and the State Department is not without the means to persuade; and the Peace Corps, with its young members' person-to-person contacts which transcend governmental activities, will be of service in overcoming misconceptions and resentments. But to change our foreign relations with Asia and Africa our symbols must change. For neither we nor they are animals: we live by our symbols as do they: we cannot change their feelings about us as long as we are acting out, symbolically, the concept of White Supremacy in schools and parks and movies and churches and buses and restaurants.

Why don't we see this? Is there a tendency to blindness in those who overvalue their whiteness? Sometimes, I think so; even in those who cannot be called racists there is blindness. If we were not blocked off by our racial feelings would we not realize that segregationists, South and North, are our country's dangerous enemies, even when unwittingly so? Would we not realize the threat they are to our survival as a strong free nation? For the sake of a mythic belief in the superiority of their "whiteness"—a strange mad obsession—they are willing to drag us to the edge of destruction because they have actually lost touch with reality. Think of the irony, the terrible absurdity of those racist U. S. Congressmen investigating everybody's subversive acts but their own—when it is what *they* are doing by their blunt, stubborn refusal to give up segregation that is pushing us closer and closer to disaster.

There are only two or three million of these racists—the other segregationists are simply conformists—but their leaders are powerful in Congress and in many southern and midwest states, powerful in certain industries, powerful in terror groups, and powerful in their hypnotic control of minds for they, by indirection, reach into mass media influencing what is written or said, thus blocking the majority of our people from a full understanding and awareness of the dangers at this moment in history.

It is such an old story. The Cassandras have been giving their warnings for years. But time has run out: we must, right now, adjust ourselves to the speed and quality of world events, world moods, world psychology or face probable extinction as a free nation.

We must—and yet, will we? So many of us are sleepwalkers wandering around in search of a past that never existed; more afraid of ghosts than of atomic war, gazing backward at a Civil War fought a century ago instead of looking into the cold eye of the storm bearing down on us.

Why are we like this? Why do so many men of my generation, born at the turn of the century, some of them in control of strategic committees in Congress, some of them Governors of southern states, some of them mayors and city commissioners, and editors and preachers—why do they feel and act as if these terrible events are not happening? Why do others continue to talk of gradualism, "moderation," "token" integration in this world emergency?

It would seem a trap in which we were hopelessly caught were it not for the young and their fine talent for doing the unpredictable. How many, even of those who have been watching for twenty-five years the awakening of Asia and Africa, foresaw the miraculous rise of the young students of the South in their nonviolent struggle for freedom? Not one. We did not dare believe they were capable of the courage and compassion, the high humor and energy they have shown. Most of them are from the Negro group but white students are joining them, sitting in, standing in, going to jail, riding the Freedom Bus "for all men's freedom and dignity." They have taken the blows of the white mob, they have had their faces smashed to a pulp, but they have not retaliated. They are not fighting *people*, they are fighting a past that bars them from a life of freedom and responsibility. For them, only the uncreated future counts: they know they must help make it. And they stand ready to suffer for the chance to do so. They believe in nonviolent ways of conciliation. "We want a future for the white man, too—not just for Negroes. We do nothing just for Negroes," their young leaders say. You remember how it began? On February 1, 1960, one student and then three more in Greensboro, North Carolina made a decision: to sit in at a lunchroom counter in a Ten Cent store which did not serve their Negro patrons. That was the small beginning. The news spread overnight across the South and soon students, Negroes mostly but a few whites, were sitting in at lunch counters and restaurants in hundreds of cities asking to be served. And words: *nonviolence, redemption, compassion, love, conciliation* were used by them as they talked together.

But it is their acting that has stirred the world: their quiet *sitting there* while burning cigarettes are pushed into their backs by white hoodlums, while they are insulted or slapped or kicked; their relaxed, amused reaction to going to jail. Few of them have succumbed to the lure of martyrdom. On the contrary, I have heard them mimic the handful of students who have dramatized a bit vividly their personal suffering. There is enormous gaiety and a fine sense of the comic which does not desert them under stress. The funniest stories I have heard in years have come from these students: in the middle of tense moments they rarely fail to see the large absurdity that keeps reducing tragedy to grim farce. There is, also, buttressing their present concern with civil rights, a deep feeling for the quality of the human experience. If this grows, if their interest in contemporary art, dance, music, poetry, drama, philosophy continues, something important and desperately needed by all of us—a new quality, a new value—can come out of these sit-in and jail-in episodes. But will it come in time? I do not know.

It is the apathy of white southerners that disturbs me; and may I add, this apathy is north and west of our region, too. There are so many people who are determined not to do wrong but equally determined not to do right. Thus they walk straight into Nothingness. Are we—the nation that first embarked on the high adventure of making a world fit for human beings to live in—about to destroy ourselves because we have killed our dream? Can we live with a dead dream inside us? How many dead dreams will it take to destroy us all?

As I write this sentence, sitting in my home in Georgia, a mob of more than a thousand white men has surrounded a Negro church in Montgomery, Alabama. It is Sunday night. Inside the Negroes are singing; they stop now and then to listen to Martin Luther King, their leader in nonviolent action, as he speaks quietly to them. Now and then, one of the other ministers speaks. The radio has just stated that Dr. King has gone into the church office to call Robert Kennedy, the United States Attorney General asking for more protection. "The mob is drawing nearer," Dr. King said quietly, "we could take a little more help."

And I sit here, listening, a white southern woman, praying that those in authority in Alabama will come to their senses, praying that all of us will come to our senses, that we will hear that voice, *We can take a little more help*.

Before this book comes off the press, there will be more incidents, more ordeals testing white and black, testing our quality as human beings, testing our wisdom. Each test will push us toward life or death.

Segregation . . . a word full of meaning for every person on earth. A word that is both symbol and symptom of our modern, fragmented world. We, the earth people, have shattered our dreams, yes; we have shattered our own lives, too, and our world. Our big problem is not civil rights nor even a free Africa—urgent as these are—but how to make into a related whole the split pieces of the human experience, how to bridge mythic and rational mind, how to connect our childhood with the present and the past with the future, how to relate the differing realities of science and religion and politics and art to each other and to ourselves. Man is a broken creature, yes; it is his nature as a human being to be so; but it is also his nature to create relationships that can span the brokenness. This is his first responsibility; when he fails, he is inevitably destroyed.

Against the sound and fury of mobs, of angry foolish defenses and flat stereotypic responses, I look at this revised version of *Killers of the Dream*, turning the manuscript pages. As I do so, children pop out of the paragraphs and some of them resemble me and my brothers and sisters. I realize this is personal memoir, in one sense; in another sense, it is Every Southerner's memoir. Childhood . . . full of absurdity and tears and laughter; but there is anguish, too, and anger at a persistent blindness that has hurt us all. Too much feeling? Perhaps. I could snip off a little of the pain, rub out a few words. But no;

let's leave it; for it may be the most real part of the book. The childhood of southerners, white and colored, has been lived on trembling earth: let us accept this, and the hurt that comes from a realization of what it means to the human spirit, and meant to me.

And now, to you, who as my editor stood by with encouragement during the first writing of it in 1948–49, who kept calm through the excitement and controversy and plain shock it aroused on publication, who never faltered in your faith in it, I return *Killers of the Dream*, smoothed and spruced up a bit, and enlarged by new paragraphs and two new chapters. I leave it, with confidence, in your hands.

Lillian Smith.

Part One

The Dreamers

1

When I Was a Child

EVEN ITS children knew that the South was in trouble. No one had to tell them; no words said aloud. To them, it was a vague thing weaving in and out of their play, like a ghost haunting an old graveyard or whispers after the household sleeps—fleeting mystery, vague menace to which each responded in his own way. Some learned to screen out all except the soft and the soothing; others denied even as they saw plainly, and heard. But all knew that under quiet words and warmth and laughter, under the slow ease and tender concern about small matters, there was a heavy burden on all of us and as heavy a refusal to confess it. The children knew this "trouble" was bigger than they, bigger than their family, bigger than their church, so big that people turned away from its size. They had seen it flash out and shatter a town's peace, had felt it tear up all they believed in. They had measured its giant strength and felt weak when they remembered.

This haunted childhood belongs to every southerner of my age. We ran away from it but we came back like a hurt animal to its wound, or a murderer to the scene of his sin. The human heart dares not stay away too long from that which hurt it most. There is a return journey to anguish that few of us are released from making.

We who were born in the South called this mesh of feeling and memory "loyalty." We thought of it sometimes as "love." We identified with the South's trouble as if we, individually, were responsible for all of it. We defended the sins and the sorrows of three hundred years as if each sin had been committed by us alone and each sorrow had cut across our heart. We were as hurt at criticism of our region as if our own name had been called aloud by the critic. We knew guilt without understanding it, and there is no tie that binds men closer to the past and each other than that.

It is a strange thing, this umbilical cord uncut. In times of ease, we do not feel its pull, but when we are threatened with change, suddenly it draws the whole white South together in a collective fear and fury that wipe our minds clear of reason and we are blocked from sensible contact with the world we live in.

To keep this resistance strong, wall after wall was thrown up in the southern mind against criticism from without and within. Imaginations closed tight against the hurt of others; a regional armoring took place to ward off the "enemies" who would make our trouble different —or maybe rid us of it completely. For it was a trouble that we did not want to give up. We were as involved with it as a child who cannot be happy at home and cannot bear to tear himself away, or as a grownup who has fallen in love with his own disease. We southerners had identified with the long sorrowful past on such deep levels of love and hate and guilt that we did not know how to break old bonds without pulling our lives down. *Change* was the evil word, a shrill clanking that made us know too well our servitude. *Change* meant leaving one's memories, one's sins, one's ambivalent pleasures, the room where one was born.

In this South I lived as a child and now live. And it is of it that my story is made. I shall not tell, here, of experiences that were different and special and belonged only to me, but those most white southerners born at the turn of the century share with each other. Out of the intricate weaving of unnumbered threads, I shall pick out a few strands, a few designs that have to do with what we call color and race . . . and politics . . . and money and how it is made . . . and religion . . . and sex and the body image . . . and love . . . and dreams of the Good and the killers of dreams.

A southern child's basic lessons were woven of such dissonant strands as these; sometimes the threads tangled into a terrifying mess; sometimes archaic, startling designs would appear in the weaving; sometimes, a design was left broken while another was completed with minute care. Bewildered teachers, bewildered pupils in home and on the street, driven by an invisible Authority, learned their lessons:

The mother who taught me what I know of tenderness and love and compassion taught me also the bleak rituals of keeping Negroes in their "place." The father who rebuked me for an air of superiority toward schoolmates from the mill and rounded out his rebuke by gravely reminding me that "all men are brothers," trained me in the steel-rigid decorums I must demand of every colored male. They who so gravely taught me to split my body from my mind and both from my "soul," taught me also to split my conscience from my acts and Christianity from southern tradition.

Neither the Negro nor sex was often discussed at length in our home. We were given no formal instruction in these difficult matters but we learned our lessons well. We learned the intricate system of taboos, of renunciations and compensations, of manners, voice modulations, words, feelings, along with our prayers, our toilet habits, and our games. I do not remember how or when, but by the time I had learned that God is love, that Jesus is His Son and came to give us more abundant life, that all men are brothers with a common Father, I also knew that I was better than a Negro, that all black folks have their place and must be kept in it, that sex has its place and must be kept in it, that a terrifying disaster would befall the South if ever I treated a Negro as my social equal and as terrifying a disaster would befall my family if ever I were to have a baby outside of marriage. I had learned that God so loved the world that He gave His only begotten Son so that we might have segregated churches in which it was my duty to worship each Sunday and on Wednesday at evening prayers. I had learned that white southerners are a hospitable, courteous, tactful people who treat those of their own group with consideration and who as carefully segregate from all the richness of life "for their own good and welfare" thirteen million people whose skin is colored a little differently from my own.

I knew by the time I was twelve that a member of my family would always shake hands with old Negro friends, would speak graciously to members of the Negro race unless they forgot their place, in which event icy peremptory tones would draw lines beyond which only the desperate would dare take one step. I knew that to use the word "nigger" was unpardonable and no well-bred southerner was quite so crude as to do so; nor would a well-bred southerner call a Negro "mister" or invite him into the living room or eat with him or sit by him in public places.

I knew that my old nurse who had cared for me through long months of illness, who had given me refuge when a little sister took my place as the baby of the family, who soothed, fed me, delighted me with her stories and games, let me fall asleep on her deep warm breast, was not worthy of the passionate love I felt for her but must be given instead a half-smiled-at affection similar to that which one feels for one's dog. I knew but I never believed it, that the deep respect I felt for her, the tenderness, the love, was a childish thing which every normal child outgrows, that such love begins with one's toys and is discarded with them, and that somehow—though it seemed impossible to my agonized heart—I too, must outgrow these feelings. I learned to use a soft voice to oil my words of superiority. I learned to cheapen with tears and sentimental talk of "my old mammy" one of the profound relationships of my life. I learned the bitterest thing a child can learn: that the human relations I valued most were held cheap by the world I lived in.

From the day I was born, I began to learn my lessons. I was put in a rigid frame too intricate, too twisting to describe here so briefly, but I learned to conform to its slide-rule measurements. I learned it is possible to be a Christian and a white southerner simultaneously; to be a gentlewoman and an arrogant callous creature in the same moment; to pray at night and ride a Jim Crow car the next morning and to feel comfortable in doing both. I learned to believe in freedom, to glow when the word *democracy* was used, and to practice slavery from morning to night. I learned it the way all of my southern people learn it: by closing door after door until one's mind and heart and conscience are blocked off from each other and from reality.

I closed the doors. Or perhaps they were closed for me. One day they began to open again. Why I had the desire or the strength to open them, or what strange accident or circumstance opened them for me would require in the answering an account too long, too particular, too stark to make here. And perhaps I should not have the wisdom that such an analysis would demand of me, nor the will to make it. I know only that the doors opened, a little; that somewhere along that iron corridor we travel

from babyhood to maturity, doors swinging inward began to swing outward, showing glimpses of the world
beyond, of that bright thing we call "reality."

I believe there is one experience which pushed these
doors open, a little. And I am going to tell it here, although I know well that to excerpt from a life and family
background one incident and name it as a "cause" of a
change in one's life direction is a distortion and often an
irrelevance. The hungers of a child and how they are
filled have too much to do with the way in which experiences are assimilated to tear an incident out of life and
look at it in isolation. Yet, with these reservations, I shall
tell it, not because it was in itself a severe trauma, but
because it became a symbol of buried experiences that I
did not have access to. It is an incident that has rarely
happened to other southern children. In a sense, unique.
But it was an acting-out, a private production of a little
script that is written on the lives of most southern children before they know words. Though they may not
have seen it staged this way, each southerner has had his
own private showing.

I should like to preface the account by giving a brief
glimpse of my family, hoping the reader, entering my
home with me, will be able to blend the edges of this
isolated experience into a more full life picture and in
doing so will see that it is, in a sense, everybody's story.

I was born and reared in a small Deep South town
whose population was about equally Negro and white.
There were nine of us who grew up freely in a rambling
house of many rooms, surrounded by big lawn, back yard,
gardens, fields, and barn. It was the kind of home that
gathers memories like dust, a place filled with laughter
and play and pain and hurt and ghosts and games. We
were given such advantages of schooling, music, and art
as were available in the South, and our world was not

limited to the South, for travel to far places seemed a natural thing to us, and usually one of the family was in a remote part of the earth.

We knew we were a respected and important family of this small town but beyond this we gave little thought to status. Our father made money in lumber and naval stores for the excitement of making and losing it—not for what money can buy nor the security which it sometimes gives. I do not remember at any time wanting "to be rich" nor do I remember that thrift and saving were ideals which our parents considered important enough to urge upon us. In the family there was acceptance of risk, a mild delight in burning bridges, an expectant "what next?" We were not irresponsible; living according to the pleasure principle was by no means our way of life. On the contrary we were trained to think that each of us should do something of genuine usefulness, and the family thought it right to make sacrifices if necessary, to give each child preparation for such work. We were also trained to think learning important, and books; but "bad" books our mother burned. We valued music and art and craftsmanship but it was people and their welfare and religion that were the foci around which our lives seemed naturally to move. Above all else, the important thing was what we "planned to do." That each of us must do something was as inevitable as breathing for we owed a "debt to society which must be paid." This was a family commandment.

While many neighbors spent their energies in counting limbs on the family tree and grafting some on now and then to give symmetry to it, or in licking scars to cure their vague malaise, or in fighting each battle and turn of battle of that Civil War which has haunted the southern conscience so long, my father was pushing his nine children straight into the future. "You have your heritage," he used to say, "some of it good, some not so good;

and as far as I know you had the usual number of grand-mothers and grandfathers. Yes, there were slaves, too many of them in the family, but that was your grand-father's mistake, not yours. The past has been lived. It is gone. The future is yours. What are you going to do with it?" He asked this question often and sometimes one knew it was but an echo of a question he had spent his life trying to answer for himself. For the future held my father's dreams; always there, not in the past, did he ex-pect to find what he had spent his life searching for.

We lived the same segregated life as did other south-erners but our parents talked in excessively Christian and democratic terms. We were told ten thousand times that status and money are unimportant (though we were well supplied with both); we were told that "all men are brothers," that we are a part of a democracy and must act like democrats. We were told that the teachings of Jesus are important and could be practiced if we tried. We were told that to be "radical" is bad, silly too; and that one must always conform to the "best behavior" of one's community and make it better if one can. We were taught that we were superior to hate and resentment, and that no member of the Smith family could stoop so low as to have an enemy. No matter what injury was done us, we must not injure ourselves further by retaliating. That was a family commandment.

We had family prayers once each day. All of us as chil-dren read the Bible in its entirety each year. We memo-rized hundreds of Bible verses and repeated them at break-fast, and said "sentence prayers" around the family table. God was not someone we met on Sunday but a permanent member of our household. It never occurred to me until I was fourteen or fifteen years old that He did not chalk up the daily score on eternity's tablets.

Despite the strain of living so intimately with God, the nine of us were strong, healthy, energetic youngsters who filled days with play and sports and music and books and managed to live most of the time on the careless level at which young lives should be lived. We had our times of anxiety of course, for there were hard lessons to be learned about the soul and "bad things" to be learned about sex. Sometimes I have wondered how we learned them with a mother so shy with words.

She was a wistful creature who loved beautiful things like lace and sunsets and flowers in a vague inarticulate way, and took good care of her children. We always knew this was not her world but one she accepted under duress. Her private world we rarely entered, though the shadow of it lay heavily on our hearts.

Our father owned large business interests, employed hundreds of colored and white laborers, paid them the prevailing low wages, worked them the prevailing long hours, built for them mill towns (Negro and white), built for each group a church, saw to it that religion was supplied free, saw to it that a commissary supplied commodities at a high price, and in general managed his affairs much as ten thousand other southern businessmen managed theirs.

Even now, I can hear him chuckling as he told my mother how he won his fight for Prohibition. The high point of the campaign was election afternoon, when he lined up the mill force of several hundred (white and black), passed out a shining silver dollar to each one, marched them in and voted liquor out of our county. It was a great day. He had won the Big Game, a game he was always playing against all kinds of evil. It did not occur to him to scrutinize the methods he used. Evil was a word written in capitals; the devil was smart; if you wanted to win you outsmarted him. It was as simple as that.

He was a hardheaded, warmhearted, high-spirited man born during the Civil War, earning his living at twelve, struggling through decades of Reconstruction and post-Reconstruction, through populist movement, through the panic of 1893, the panic of 1907, on into the twentieth century accepting his region as he found it, accepting its morals and its mores as he accepted its climate, with only scorn for those who held grudges against the North or pitied themselves or the South; scheming, dreaming, expanding his business, making and losing money, making friends whom he did not lose, with never a doubt that God was by his side whispering hunches as to how to pull off successful deals. When he lost, it was his own fault. When he won, God had helped him.

Once while we were kneeling at family prayers the fire siren at the mill sounded the alarm that the mill was on fire. My father did not falter. The alarm sounded again and again—which signified the fire was big. With dignity he continued his talk with God while his children sweated and wriggled and hearts beat out of their chests in excitement. He was talking to God—how could he hurry out to save his mills! When he finished his prayer, he quietly stood up, laid the Bible carefully on the table. Then, and only then, did he show an interest in what was happening in Mill Town. . . . When the telegram was placed in his hands telling of the death of his beloved favorite son, he gathered his children together, knelt down, and in a steady voice which contained no hint of his shattered heart, loyally repeated, "God is our refuge and strength, a very present help in trouble. Therefore will we not fear, though the earth be removed, and though the mountains be carried into the midst of the sea." On his deathbed, he whispered to his old Business Partner in Heaven: "I have fought a good fight . . . I have kept the faith."

Against this backdrop the drama of the South was played out one day in my life:

A little white girl was found in the colored section of

our town, living with a Negro family in a broken-down shack. This family had moved in a few weeks before and little was known of them. One of the ladies in my mother's club, while driving over to her washerwoman's, saw the child swinging on a gate. The shack, as she said, was hardly more than a pigsty and this white child was living with dirty and sick-looking colored folks. "They must have kidnapped her," she told her friends. Genuinely shocked, the clubwomen busied themselves in an attempt to do something, for the child was very white indeed. The strange Negroes were subjected to a grueling questioning and finally grew evasive and refused to talk at all. This only increased the suspicion of the white group. The next day the clubwomen, escorted by the town marshal, took the child from her adopted family despite their tears.

She was brought to our home. I do not know why my mother consented to this plan. Perhaps because she loved children and always showed concern for them. It was easy for one more to fit into our ample household and Janie was soon at home there. She roomed with me, sat next to me at the table; I found Bible verses for her to say at breakfast; she wore my clothes, played with my dolls and followed me around from morning to night. She was dazed by her new comforts and by the interesting activities of this big lively family; and I was as happily dazed, for her adoration was a new thing to me; and as time passed a quick, childish, and deeply felt bond grew up between us.

But a day came when a telephone message was received from a colored orphanage. There was a meeting at our home. Many whispers. All afternoon the ladies went in and out of our house talking to Mother in tones too low for children to hear. As they passed us at play, they looked at Janie and quickly looked away again, though a few stopped and stared at her as if they could not tear their eyes from her face. When my father came home

Mother closed her door against our young ears and talked a long time with him. I heard him laugh, heard Mother say, "But Papa, this is no laughing matter!" And then they were back in the living room with us and my mother was pale and my father was saying, "Well, work it out, Mame, as best you can. After all, now that you know, it is pretty simple."

In a little while my mother called my sister and me into her bedroom and told us that in the morning Janie would return to Colored Town. She said Janie was to have the dresses the ladies had given her and a few of my own, and the toys we had shared with her. She asked me if I would like to give Janie one of my dolls. She seemed hurried, though Janie was not to leave until next day. She said, "Why not select it now?" And in dreamlike stiffness I brought in my dolls and chose one for Janie. And then I found it possible to say, "Why is she leaving? She likes us, she hardly knows them. She told me she had been with them only a month."

"Because," Mother said gently, "Janie is a little colored girl."

"But she's white!"

"We were mistaken. She is colored."

"But she looks—"

"She is colored. Please don't argue!"

"What does it mean?" I whispered.

"It means," Mother said slowly, "that she has to live in Colored Town with colored people."

"But why? She lived here three weeks and she doesn't belong to them, she told me so."

"She is a little colored girl."

"But you said yourself she has nice manners. You said that," I persisted.

"Yes, she is a nice child. But a colored child cannot live in our home."

"Why?"

"You know, dear! You have always known that white and colored people do not live together."

"Can she come to play?"

"No."

"I don't understand."

"I don't either," my young sister quavered.

"You're too young to understand. And don't ask me again, ever again, about this!" Mother's voice was sharp but her face was sad and there was no certainty left there. She hurried out and busied herself in the kitchen and I wandered through that room where I had been born, touching the old familiar things in it, looking at them, trying to find the answer to a question that moaned like a hurt thing. . . .

And then I went out to Janie, who was waiting, knowing things were happening that concerned her but waiting until they were spoken aloud.

I do not know quite how the words were said but I told her she was to return in the morning to the little place where she had lived because she was colored and colored children could not live with white children.

"Are you white?" she said.

"I'm white," I replied, "and my sister is white. And you're colored. And white and colored can't live together because my mother says so."

"Why?" Janie whispered.

"Because they can't," I said. But I knew, though I said it firmly, that something was wrong. I knew my father and mother whom I passionately admired had betrayed something which they held dear. And they could not help doing it. And I was shamed by their failure and frightened, for I felt they were no longer as powerful as I had thought. There was something Out There that was stronger than they and I could not bear to believe it. I could not confess that my father, who always solved the family dilemmas easily and with laughter, could not solve this. I knew that my mother who was so good to children did not believe in her heart that she was being good to this child. There was not a word in my mind that said it but my body knew and my glands, and I was filled with anxiety.

But I felt compelled to believe they were right. It was the only way my world could be held together. And, slowly, it began to seep through me: *I was white. She was colored. We must not be together. It was bad to be together. Though you ate with your nurse when you were little, it was bad to eat with any colored person after that. It was bad just as other things were bad that your mother had told you. It was bad that she was to sleep in the room with me that night. It was bad. . . .*

I was overcome with guilt. For three weeks I had done things that white children were not supposed to do. And now I knew these things had been wrong.

I went to the piano and began to play, as I had always done when I was in trouble. I tried to play my next lesson and as I stumbled through it, the little girl came over and sat on the bench with me. Feeling lost in the deep currents sweeping through our house that night, she crept closer and put her arms around me and I shrank away as if my body had been uncovered. I had not said a word, I did not say one, but she knew, and tears slowly rolled down her little white face. . . .

And then I forgot it. For more than thirty years the experience was wiped out of my memory. But that night, and the weeks it was tied to, worked its way like a splinter, bit by bit, down to the hurt places in my memory and festered there. And as I grew older, as more experiences collected around that faithless time, as memories of earlier, more profound hurts crept closer, drawn to that night as if to a magnet, I began to know that people who talked of love and children did not mean it. That is a hard thing for a child to learn. I still admired my parents, there was so much that was strong and vital and sane and good about them and I never forgot this; I stubbornly believed in their sincerity, as I do to this day, and I loved them. Yet in my heart they were under suspicion. Something was wrong.

Something was wrong with a world that tells you that love is good and people are important and then forces you to deny love and to humiliate people. I knew, though I would not for years confess it aloud, that in trying to shut the Negro race away from us, we have shut ourselves away from so many good, creative, honest, deeply human things in life. I began to understand slowly at first but more clearly as the years passed, that the warped, distorted frame we have put around every Negro child from birth is around every white child also. Each is on a different side of the frame but each is pinioned there. And I knew that what cruelly shapes and cripples the personality of one is as cruelly shaping and crippling the personality of the other. I began to see that though we may, as we acquire new knowledge, live through new experiences, examine old memories, gain the strength to tear the frame from us, yet we are stunted and warped and in ✳ our lifetime cannot grow straight again any more than can a tree, put in a steel-like twisting frame when young, grow tall and straight when the frame is torn away at maturity.

As I sit here writing, I can almost touch that little town, so close is the memory of it. There it lies, its main street lined with great oaks, heavy with matted moss that swings softly even now as I remember. A little white town rimmed with Negroes, making a deep shadow on the whiteness. There it lies, broken in two by one strange idea. Minds broken. Hearts broken. Conscience torn from acts. A culture split in a thousand pieces. That is segregation. *mental illness* I am remembering: a woman in a mental hospital walking four steps out, four steps in, unable to go further because she has drawn an invisible line around her small world and is terrified to take one step beyond it. . . . A man in a Disturbed Ward assigning "places" to the other patients and violently insisting that each stay in his place. . . . A Negro woman saying to me so quietly, "We cannot ride together on the bus, you know. It is not legal to be human down here."

Memory, walking the streets of one's childhood . . . of the town where one was born.

2

Custom and Conscience

THAT WAS long ago.

In the South, paint has peeled off of old houses we were born in; steps have sagged down. Foundations of economics and politics and old ways of living have crumbled though the rotted framework stands. The new has begun. Housing projects and ranch houses shut out the sight of the old big houses and shanties. People have moved to town. There is more money. Tractors and bulldozers, cover crops and contour plowing have filled deep gullies and made green pastures of worn-out land. Factories are building in small-town vacant lots where we children played ball or in springtime picked yellow flycatchers from little damp places. Unions hold their meetings in old second-story rooms where lodges once met for their conclaves. Motels and filling stations, chain restaurants, hot-dog stands and gift shops edge the broad black strip that has unrolled across clay and sand and swamp and hill.

How far away it seems now since that old horse-and-buggy clop clop of years made childhood so painful and wondrous a time of slow watching! Those old crowded years when eyes had time to look seem now as if they moved under a microscope.

On that dreary evening, when I wandered through our

big house trying to fit good and evil into something that made sense, there was not one automobile in our town. Few people had heard of Kitty Hawk and the brothers who had learned to fly. I remember the day the first telephone came to our town. The night the first electric lights were turned on. The first flush toilet that was installed in my mother's bathroom.

During these many years since I was a little girl struggling with conscience and custom, this old earth has seen more change in men's ways than in thousands of years of its history.

One keeps turning the pages. . . . In Europe, Sigmund Freud was already embattled by the fear and hatred of men who recognized too well the power of his findings, but we had not heard of him in the South or in most of America. No one had begun to worry about the hidden terror in the unconscious; no one apparently guessed that children had a sex life though Stendhal had written his biography and Dostoievsky his novels and Rousseau his confessions and the old Greek plays had been acted thousands of times in the Western world. Insanity might be upstairs in the room whose door was always kept closed but no one talked of it and no one believed it could be otherwise. . . . Few knew the names of Einstein and Planck or had read the words *quantum theory*, and atomic energy was a vague daydream that men put in escape stories. Many in the rural South had not yet heard of Marx, and evolution was to most southern people not controversy but a sin that only infidels or those who believed in the "Higher Criticism" dared even read about.

In a corner of Austria the greatest murderer the world has ever known was living his childhood; Stalin was a young peasant in that beautiful old province on the Black Sea that has a name like ours; and the adolescent Kafka was beginning his terrifying trials that drove him, years later, to write down anxiety dreams that we shiveringly claim as our own now as we read them; Picasso had not learned yet to lay the thin slivers of a broken world in blocks of color so hypnotic with ugliness and strange truth that men can scarcely pull their eyes from the sight of it, though his culture had already shown him how, but was still dipping his brush in misty blues and dreaming of a whole person who no longer existed. In South Africa, Gandhi was weaving a way of change out of nonviolence and love and *satyagraha* which decades later would free four hundred million of his people in India. The Soongs were obscure Methodists whose best friends were missionaries; Chiang Kai-shek was a peasant boy in his teens riding the family's buffalo home in the evenings across rice paddies that lay shadowed by the mountains of Chekiang; and Franklin Roosevelt was a young college man spending carefree summers on the island of Campobello. Strangers one to another, distant and remote . . . yet all were being pulled inexorably together and we were pulled with them by men in laboratories, who wrapped their invisible theories around the old earth tighter and tighter and squeezed it into so small a thing that even now we cannot believe it.

Even now, in the South, we still try to live as if none of this has happened. The old signs are still over the minds of men. Custom and conscience still divide our children and southern tradition is a ghost that many still believe in.

I saw a group of southern children try their strength against that ghost a few summers ago. It happened on our mountain where the children were spending the summer. We were gathered in the big gymnasium-theater making a play. It was the children's affair and was about Every Child who makes a journey through the universe to collect new experiences he may need in order to grow up. They had read Antoine de Saint Exupéry's fantasy *The Little Prince* and, borrowing from it, had agreed that in their play Every Child was born on a planet, too, where no one lives but himself but if he grows he does not stay there. There are other planets which he must visit. In such simple pictures they saw the old troubled story of man's progress. A camper was chosen for the role of Every Child and given the name the Prince. The first planet to be visited on this journey was Your Own Family. The Prince's first traveling companion joined him here and the campers named her Conscience, made her into a tall nurse-maid, prissy and prudish, and designed a bristling costume for her that contained surely all the angularities of their combined early experiences.

The Prince had begun his journey. The second experience was concerned with the weaning from the nipple to the cup. There were others: the first day at school, getting rid of one's fear of the dark, making a friend, creating things with one's hands. As the play grew, the children realized that the Prince must have more traveling companions—Conscience did not seem adequate for so hazardous a journey. So Southern Tradition was chosen as his second companion, and a group of eight dancers were to stay close to the Prince, blocking his way or opening it, as he traveled. The third companion they chose was Religion. "I know we should take religion along," one child said, "but it just doesn't seem to belong on the stage with the others—after all, it's near us only on Sundays."

"Then put it in the balcony," another called out. And they did, asking five girls to take their Bibles to the far balcony and sit there.

The fourth companion chosen was Science. It was not easy to convince the group that the Prince needed this traveling companion. But Science had one ardent defender. A quiet, withdrawn girl now spoke. "We live in the age of science," she said, "and we shouldn't make a journey through the universe with only a nursemaid like Conscience, and Southern Tradition and Religion. It's too dangerous. There are times when the Prince better know some facts."

"Yes, but what about? He can't take things like refrigerators with him on a journey through the universe!"

"Things aren't science," the quiet camper replied. "Science makes things, but," she groped for words, "it is really the search for truth. It's not easy to find truth, for you must test it and test it. The Prince may need the truth if he gets far from home. I think we'd better let Science help him find it."

Science was reluctantly chosen and put on the other balcony opposite religion. The Prince continued his journey.

Now we were in trouble. The Prince was speaking new words. She said, "I was born on a planet where I live all alone. I have journeyed to other planets and have had strange and wonderful experiences. I have lived with my family. I have gone to school. I have felt lonely and I have failed. But I am no longer afraid of the dark and there are things I know that once I did not know. I have made things with my hands. I have also made a friend and that was nice and I shall never forget it. I have had a date. I have family memories that are good and some I hate to remember and all of them I take with me wherever I journey."

She looked up quickly at the campers and counselors who were watching the play grow. "Last night," she continued, "I thought, Here we are making a play about visiting planets and have forgot that we live on a planet called Earth. It is a star hanging in the sky and must seem a pretty thing to the rest of the universe but I haven't traveled far on it and I don't know anything much about its people. Most of it is cut off from me and part of my town is cut off, too. We are children living on the earth and I think to grow up we should play with all the earth's children. That is an important experience which the

Prince in our play has never had. Don't you think he should have it?"

For a long moment no one answered. Then a youngster burst out, "Yes, but you know we can't play with all children! It will ruin our play. We can't have a happy ending if we do that."

Voices were angry as one after another had something to say. "You know this. Why did you mention it?"

"Why can't we end it with a nice experience that isn't controversial?"

"Something we can really do!"

"Why bring up things—"

The little Prince said, "But this journey through the universe means having experiences that will make us grow up. We've talked about it for three or four summers. The Prince has to play with other children, you know that. He's got to be interested in everybody. What's the sense of making this journey if he doesn't meet all kinds of people? Is he going to see just white people like us here at camp? He might as well sit at home."

"Then for goodness sakes, let him play with the French or somebody safe!"

"It wouldn't be honest! If he plays with children he must play with those in mill town and colored ones too, right here in Georgia."

"Oh my goodness! Then we can't. And you know it. Why be so silly!"

"Down here we just can't—"

"Daddy says—"

"My mother says—"

The old battle of words was on and the accent was very southern. The gong sounded for lunch. Quiet Hour came. Then swimming, tennis, other activities. We did not return to the play until next day. When the group was seated, I suggested that we talk about it as people who don't give up something they want just because things get hard. "Yesterday, everybody was excited. Today well, let's see what the four traveling companions can suggest. After all, that's what they're for, isn't it?"

The actors had made their own lines from the beginning of the play. Now one of them said, "Shall we make our words or will you help us? You know, since this is a kind of emergency."

"Make your own lines. As honestly as you can."

The Prince's eyes were bright as she stepped out to the center of the stage. "I am an earth child," she said proudly, "and this is a planet I live on. I would like to play with all its children for I, too, am its child."

The children who were not in the play sat on the floor, watching. On the stage were Conscience the nursemaid and the eight girls who were Southern Tradition. On the two balconies were Religion and Science. Both balcony groups had come to the play-making with armfuls of books, to meet this emergency.

A child from the floor spoke. "We can still get out of this mess if Conscience will only tell the Prince that we can't play with other children because we don't know their games."

"But we do," the Prince said. "All children play with balls and chase each other. If they don't they can learn in five minutes. That's a tricky way out and I won't use it." She turned quickly to Conscience. "Conscience, will you let me play with the colored children here at home?" In an aside to us, "We might as well get to the point, don't you think?"

Conscience ad-libbed her lines. "Don't be silly," she replied calmly. "When race is the issue I always refer you to Southern Tradition. You know that. Why don't you ask her?" Southern Tradition's eight girls blocked the Prince's path. "This is our answer," their leader said. "If you try it, we will hurt you."

The Prince's cheeks flushed up. A little seven-year-old

covered her eyes. Each camper in that room was living this play now as if it were her own biography.

The Prince turned to me, "What next?"

"You have other resources. See what Religion says."

The girls in Religion's balcony were ready. They read in chorus a part of the Sermon on the Mount. They read, "For God so loved the world, that He gave His only begotten Son. . . ." And then one girl said with such simplicity that it was truly moving, "Suffer little children to come unto me, and forbid them not: for of such is the kingdom of God."

"Conscience, did you hear?"

Conscience turned away arrogantly, "I never listen to Religion where segregation is involved. No one does, down here."

As Conscience answered, the eight who were Southern Tradition had quickly encircled the Prince and now were forcing her back from her journey toward the earth children.

"I think," a youngster called out from among those watching, "that Religion is no good as a traveling companion as long as it stays up in the balcony. Why doesn't Religion come down here and push Custom back where it belongs?"

"But Religion doesn't do that in the South," a girl from the balcony answered. "Religion stays out of controversies. You know that. Our place is up here."

"How about Science?" I asked.

The five who were Science had their answers and gave them, but even as they talked, Conscience turned away in great boredom. "I can't hear Science's words. The only thing that Science is good for is to make things like bombs and planes. Anyway, this isn't my affair. It is Southern Tradition's."

"You haven't a chance," a nine-year-old camper called out to the Prince in great excitement. "Religion's way off on her balcony, reading the Bible. Science is way off on its balcony, making things and writing books. They're not worth a thing as traveling companions! You may as well give up. Southern Tradition is too strong."

The Prince had begun to run. She twisted and turned, ran quickly, ran slowly; yet always the eight who were Southern Tradition blocked her way. She lost herself in her struggle, stopped acting, and finally I called to her to stop, fearing she would exhaust herself. She fell on the floor, breathing hard, and lay there, staring up at the ceiling.

I can never forget that moment. I looked at the children. They sat so still, a hundred campers and counselors, looking at something they had never seen before. And I sat there, remembering a day long ago that I had forgotten.

"The little Prince can never grow up," one said softly.

"Maybe we shouldn't have tried. Maybe it would have been better if the little Prince had stayed in Saint Exupéry's book."

"I knew yesterday something bad was about to happen! Why did the Prince feel that we must play with all the earth's children? You knew we couldn't do it!"

"Because," the Prince answered, doggedly, "the Prince in our play wants to do right. We know it is right to feel this way. *Our* conscience has changed whether the one in the play has or not. There should be a way to work it out. Religion and Science should have helped me; I wasn't strong enough to do it by myself."

"But they couldn't—honestly! This is the way the traveling companions are in the South. This is the way Conscience is too. We can't pretend a lie," Conscience hotly defended herself and the others.

The play had to be mended. I told them that things were as their actors had said but things need not be that way. A day would come soon when the little Prince could

play with the earth's children. Therefore it seemed to me
that we might bridge over the gap in time. We could let
Religion come down from the balcony and help. But I
felt we must decide first what religion is. Is it reading the
Bible and singing hymns and being Protestant or Catholic
or Jew or Christian Scientist, or is it something more important?

Everyone was again talking, eager to find a way out of
this impasse which they themselves had created. Religion
is love, an older girl said; no one has dreamed of anything
better than love, so it must be love. "Yes, it is love," the
little ones chimed in, relieved that the talk was growing
pleasant. Love, they continued, can help push Southern
Tradition off the stage and teach it a few lessons about
being nice to other people if Science will come down
from its balcony to help.

Quickly the young scientists came down and joined the
Prince. Quickly they improvised a dance in which they
drove Southern Tradition—nonviolently of course!—into
the wings of the stage, then they turned on Conscience.
They told her she was a coward always to listen to Southern Tradition: why couldn't she learn things from Religion and Science! And then, the campers watching this,
decided they could impersonate earth children, they could
be Chinese and Japanese and Germans and Russians and
Negroes, they could come from the ends of the earth
and play with the little Prince. And they did this. A coun-
selor put a gay record on the machine and the old gym-
nasium filled with sounds of triumph as we made a great
circle and danced together.

It was make-believe and we knew it. But we could not
let our play die as so much that is young has died on that
old wall, segregation. At supper, the children looked
tired and preoccupied and I knew we had not answered
the question twisting in their minds.

Late that evening, long after the lights in the cabins were out, a camper came into my office. She was an older girl who had spent many summers on the mountain, now ready for college in the fall. She was pale and tense, as she began to talk. I did not record that conversation but it has fixed itself in my mind so deeply that I do not think I shall distort its truth as I tell it now.

"I don't know how to begin; I shock myself as I try." She faltered and then the words rushed from her, "I think you have done a terrible thing to children."

"Why do you think so?"

"You see," she was sorting the words that had piled up in her, "you have made us want to be good. *Mature*, you've called it. You taught us to be honest, not to cover up things. You made us think it fine to be like that, even when it hurt. All these years, you've said so much about human dignity—it's a nice phrase. . . . You've talked of love . . . human rights . . . bridging chasms between people—

"But it's all wrong! You made us think of ourselves as no better than other people. You shouldn't have done that. Oh, I can't find my words, the feelings are too close here," she touched her throat.

"Perhaps you would like to wait and tell me tomorrow."

"No. I'd lose my nerve. You told us we were like children everywhere; that money and color, the church you go to, don't make any difference. And the kids believed you. You said the only real differences have to do with values and interests and tastes. And you said that the most precious right a human has is his right to be different. Even his right to be dull." She smiled suddenly. "We liked that. And we believed you. We loved you for giving us ideals that we could be proud of. We wanted to live them. They seemed so fine." She laughed a bitter little laugh, then added softly, "But I almost hate you to-night, for letting us fall in love with beliefs that I see now we can't possibly live. Why did you teach us to want to be real persons when you knew there was no place down here for such people?

"When I go back to my town, how can I live these ideals! Tell me, if you can—but you can't! That's what I have just realized.

"I saw it as we worked on the play. For the first time in my life! I guess you've tried to tell us but somehow I didn't see it. It always seemed something we could do—when we were grown. Well, I see now. And I think the others saw it too, though most are too young to find words for their feelings. Maybe they're lucky."

She came close to my desk. "It was as if somebody had swung a bright mirror in front of us. The whole thing opened up! How it would be—if we tried to live the way we have learned to want to live. Can't you imagine my town—if I were to go home and invite a colored girl to Sunday school? Or even try to get one of the girls in Mill Town in my sorority? They'd think I was crazy. Suppose I said to a colored girl, 'Let's go in the drugstore and have a coke'? Can't you see their faces—Mother's and Daddy's—and everybody's! Well, I can—especially if they arrested me and put me in jail.

"I'd be breaking a law, wouldn't I, if I tried to live these ideals in my home town?"

"Yes. You would be breaking a law. A state law."

"Do you think we should break laws? Do you *want* us to be lawbreakers? Oh, I know! I even know I could break the law and they wouldn't dare put me in jail, be-cause of Daddy. But that only makes it worse, for they would put others there. We forgot to take law along as a traveling companion, didn't we? Maybe it's better. It might make the little ones wonder if *anybody* has any sense down here.

"I'm saying these things because I'm scared—at what I am looking at in me."

She said no more for a little and I did not try to talk.

"Who put those signs over doors?" she asked suddenly. "Somebody must keep them there. Is it my father? He owns a textile mill and hates the FEPC. No, don't tell me. I don't want to know if he has anything to do with it— I couldn't believe it—he's so good—I've never seen Daddy do an unkind thing in all my life. Sometimes Mother loses her temper. Not Daddy. Then *why* does he want to keep Negroes segregated—what pleasure does he get out of it? Does it make him richer to keep them that way?"

"Some people think so."

"But why does he care that much for money? Why would he be willing to—" She said no more for what seemed a long time. I was searching hard for the right answer to give her.

She said more quietly, "Mother reads the *Nation* and the *New Republic*. All those papers. I wonder why. . . . If they've made up their minds that the signs stay up and segregation is going to be here forever, then why do they fool themselves? Why don't they be honest about it? Why pretend and go to church and say nice words? It doesn't make sense! What does religion mean to them? If it isn't real, what do they get out of it?

"I've been here six summers. I love this old mountain . . . the courtesy every one shows children; even the little ones. It's nice. We laugh so much here. . . . I've learned to paint and my drive has improved in tennis; I can even dance, a little. And the idea of growing—I've liked that. The way we've learned to think our bodies are honorable. No shame. . . . I remember you said freedom and responsibility are like Siamese twins: they die if they are cut apart. . . . All these things. . . . No punishment . . . just understanding . . . reaching out to accept other people as human beings like ourselves. We've all said we were going to bring up our children that way.

"I remember when we learned about hate. I was so afraid of that word—I used to deny that I hated anyone. And then, one day, you told us that human relationships are what the personality is fed on: love is the part you grow on, hate the part you don't need, the waste that is excreted. You said our job is to find sanitary ways of getting rid of it so it won't harm others, or ourselves. That was such a relief, to know that hate is as natural as a b.m. and much the same thing. I stopped biting my nails when I learned that." She smiled and looked down at her hands. "I remember all the Sunday mornings we've discussed these things, sitting under the trees."

I said, "You think it's wrong—what we have learned here together?"

"I think it's useless. It just tears us up inside! Makes us so raw. Oh, I hate to say it, but I do think you have harmed us. You've unfitted us for the South. And yet, this is where we shall live. Unless we run away.

"I think you should have made it easier for us to live here. What is education for if not that! Since we have to practice segregation, why didn't you make us think it is right?"

"How could it be right?"

"Oh, I don't know! My mind feels as if it is full of barbed wire. It isn't right for any one to feel the way I feel—inside.

"When I have children, I am not going to give them a single ideal they can't practice. I don't want them torn up like this. I'll tell them Jim Crow is fine, that it's legal, that this is the way things are in the South and the way they are going to stay. I'll tell them they have the right to push folks around; that they *should* decide where their inferiors can sit and stand and what doors they can go through. That it's right to shame colored children by making them go through back doors."

She came to my desk. "I haven't told you about last

winter.* Daddy took me to New York—we were in the dining car—had just finished our soup—when I saw the steward seat the president of that college in Atlanta behind those curtains. I had heard him make a speech at a church meeting. I said, 'Daddy, did you see that? He's the president of a college!' And Daddy said, 'That's where colored folks are supposed to sit. You mustn't get silly notions, honey.' I couldn't finish my dinner. I know it was morbid, but I kept looking at all those faces wondering why they felt they had to have a curtain between them and the president of a college, just to eat their dinner. And it began to seem so crazy!

"I'll teach my children not to *think* about things like this. I'll teach them that money comes first, before people, that it's more important. I won't let them be hypocrites, like me."

"In other words, you would make little Nazis out of them."

"At least it would be honest!"

"I'm afraid honesty doesn't have much to do with it, though it would be logical. Your feelings have stampeded a little, haven't they?"

"I'm scared," she whispered. "I don't like the future. It doesn't seem to belong to us. I don't know what to believe about anything. I'm seventeen years old and I have no idea what is wrong and what is right—not enough to know how to live. And even if I knew, I couldn't live it down here. I lay there tonight trying to tell myself that segregation is right. I said it over and over as I used to do as a child when I was memorizing. I said 'Daddy knows more than we know here at camp. There's no sense in worrying about it.' But it didn't help.

"You see," her voice had quieted, "I want so much to go home and be decent about things. Not make folks mad

* 1961. There is no segregation in dining cars in the South now, if these cars are used in interstate travel.

Author's note.

—just live what I believe is right. But how? Tell me how! What shall I do when I get on a bus—go to the front with the white folks? Or shall I speak to the bus driver and make a little scene each time I get on? Shall I keep on going through White doors? Can I persuade my class to invite a colored girl to Sunday school? Suppose I get that far—will the minister let me? I don't think he would— he would say, 'These things have to come slowly, my dear,' and he would mean that they must not come at all, as long as there is any risk in it. If I do these things that seem so important to us up here, everybody at home will be furious. I can't take it."

"What are you afraid of?"

"I don't know. It's like waking up in the night after a dream—you're just scared, you don't know why. I just can't fight people I love. Maybe it's because I want to be liked too much. But it's right to want people to like you, isn't it?"

"Yes," I was feeling old, "it's right to want people to like you."

"Funny," she said, "I don't want to hate and I don't want people to hate me. That ought to be a good way to feel. But you won't change things down here if you feel that way. Do you remember the book you gave me to read on the well-adjusted child? Well, that's me—I'm beginning to see it. I'm just too easygoing. To change things you've got to get mad when you see folks do what you think is wrong. But I can't stand people who shout and scream and push others around in the name of good. They seem crazy. And I don't want anybody calling *me* a crack-pot—that's what Daddy calls people.

"It makes you feel tired inside to think things like this," she turned away to hide her tears.

I said, "I would like for you to let me talk a little now. And I have to begin before you were born."

And then I told her in part what I shall write down here in the next chapter.

3

Unto the Third and Fourth Generation

"YOU HAVE to remember," I said, "that the trouble we are in started long ago. Your parents didn't make it, nor I. We were born into it. Signs were put over doors when we were babies. We took them for granted just as we took heat and sandspurs and mosquitoes. We worried about things close to home but I don't think we noticed the signs. Somehow we seemed always to walk through the right door. People find it hard to question something that has been here since they were born.

"Before these signs went up, there had been a war in which people were killed, homes burned that held a family's memories. That isn't an easy thing to forget. Before that war, there had been a way of living that destroyed human dignity, and for a long time people in the South did not even think those words. These were evil experiences for white and Negro, rich and poor, but they were curiously complicated by the attitude of the North and South toward each other.

"Perhaps the best way to explain that attitude is to

think of two brothers, each of whom is 'on the make,' each of whom is greedy, and ruthless in his determination to make money. But one makes his money easily, having figured a way to let others do it for him, and spends it lavishly on a gracious, luxurious life for his family; and having more leisure, he becomes more urbane, and 'charming' and his life more and more gay and pleasant, and without toil, while his wife is surrounded by servants who do everything for her. The other brother is industrious, his wife does the housework, he saves more, invests it shrewdly, considers himself more provident and 'sensible' than his brother but all the time he secretly envies his brother's sins for they seem more fun than his own and he covets his dominant power in the family's affairs. Feeling this way, he begins to think a great deal about his brother's sins. It bothers him that his brother doesn't pay wages to his laborers. He does not pay much himself but he at least pays a little. And this makes him feel self-righteous. At the same time, he feels that his morals handicap him.

"Then things change. Machines are invented. The industrious brother, keeping wages down to a low level, begins to make money by building factories. As he gains in wealth and power, his brother on the farm finds it less easy to make a living even with slave labor. Each now begins to fight the other, for each wants to hold the balance of power in the family. Each insists that his way of making a living is best and tries to force his way on the rest of the family.

"The brother who has made money so easily with slave labor watches his income dwindle year after year as compared to his brother's income which is doubling and quadrupling as more factories are built, and in his frustration, he declares that he is going to withdraw from the family unless his brother stops criticising him. The hardworking brother, still jealous, and just as greedy as the brother he has criticised so long, is shocked and declares that nothing can break up a family; no generation, however sharp its differences, has the right to tear a family to pieces. The argument shifts now and is concerned with this 'right' to withdraw and feelings grow more bitter. It is not long, with tempers so hot, before the two brothers are in terrible conflict and the rest of the family is forced to take sides with one or the other.

"Such feelings as these between North and South make it impossible, even today, to say in a few words what the Civil War was about. It was about greed, and two systems that could not exist in the same country, and a lust for political power. It had to do with a region's right to withdraw when it has quarreled with the rest of the nation. But regardless of *states' rights* and *union*, and competing economic systems, and the struggle for power in Congress, the war would not have been fought had there not been slavery.

"In the North, there was throughout these decades of conflict, a group of honest, thoughtful men and women who sincerely loved human freedom, who knew slavery would destroy the integrity not only of our democratic institutions but of our Christian people, whose hearts were stirred by the cruelties of the slave system in the South, and who spoke out at this time solely because of their concern for the Negro and his human rights. These were the abolitionists, a courageous group of idealists whose words sprang from deep beliefs. The part of the North that was fighting for political power unscrupulously exploited them, using their words as a weapon to wage a holy war against the South by arousing the conscience of idealists at the same time that they stirred the patriotism of others over the threatened partition of their country.

"Our South understood these motives and was shaken by a terrible anger. The North's moral arguments were

so obviously right; its desires so selfish. Southerners responded by as wild and arrogant and angry a defense as
a hotheaded people could give. It is only by trying to
understand these mixed feelings made of ideals and greed
and power-lust and patriotism and regional jealousy that
we can understand the feelings which, even today, shrewd
politicians, North and South, exploit to their own advantage. There is still self-righteousness in the North and
hatred of the 'dam-yankee' in the South.

"Then the war came. And the South lost everything
it cherished. And for a little while there was no room
for hate in most men's hearts, for there was so much
sadness. The whole region mourned its dead, its loss, its
deep hurt. Sometimes the little things were the hardest
to bear: a broken old tree under which one had played in
childhood, charred camellias and boxwoods. . . . The
ruins were so vast that only by finding a small loss to
hover over could the heart endure its emptiness. A mel-
ancholy fell on minds and was never lifted from some of
them. And then the terrible, the unforeseen happened:
President Lincoln was killed by a southerner. A neurotic,
unstable actor was the murderer but he was southern.
The North's feelings that day and the next and the next
were just what our country's would have been had a
German assassinated Roosevelt.

"After Lincoln's tragic death, northern pulpits and
press lost all objectivity and in righteous wrath demanded
that the whole South be punished for this crime. Now
once more the North was condemning us. They called
the South a Problem, they called its people 'barbarians,'
they insisted that this proud people be humbled. They
blamed us for the terrible Reconstruction which followed; they blamed us for their own lack of planning
and vision; they blamed us for the failures of their Freedmen's Bureau—which in spite of its muddle-headed seven
years of existence did a good and terribly needed job of

helping more than four million ex-slaves find a life as freedmen. They hung our racial sins up for the world to look at, and at the same time began to practice these sins, under cover, up North. They blamed and grew rich and smug, and we hated and grew poor and stubborn.

"Hypocrisy, greed, self-righteousnes, defensiveness twisted in men's minds. The South grew more sensitive to criticism, more defensive and dishonest in its thinking. For deep down in their hearts, southerners knew they were wrong. They knew it in slavery just as they later knew that sharecropping was wrong, and as they know today that segregation is wrong. It was not only the North's criticism that made them defensive, it was their own conscience. Our grandparents called themselves Christians and sometimes believed they were. Believing it, they were compelled to believe it was morally right for them to hold slaves. They could not say, 'We shall keep our slaves because they are profitable, regardless of right and wrong.' A few tough old realists who didn't claim to be in the Fold probably did say it. But to most, such words would have seemed as fantastic as a confession of their mixed reasons for opposing slavery would have seemed to the Yankees. Our grandfathers' conscience compelled them to justify slavery and they did: by making the black man 'different,' setting him outside God's law, reducing him to less than human. In a way that would have seemed blasphemous, had they stopped to think, they took God's place and 'decided' which of His creatures have souls and which do not. And once doing it, they continued doing it, and their sons continued doing it, and their grandsons, telling themselves and their children more and more and more lies about white superiority until they no longer knew the truth and were lost in a maze of fantasy and falsehood that had little resemblance to the actual world they lived in.

"It's a strange thing how a man's own conscience can

trap his soul. North and South, this happened.

"But the lies and defenses and fabulous justifications did not keep our people from feeling guilty; and feeling it, they felt also a need to suffer, and like guilty people everywhere, they had to find 'enemies' to be punished by. The 'dam-yankee' was the perfect psychological enemy, for had not this Yankee unjustly blamed the South for a sin he too had committed in another form! And had not this Yankee 'unjustly punished' the whole South for this sin! And was not this Yankee even today 'persecuting' the South!

"The North felt guilty, also, for its greed and its hypocritical lying and the damage that had been done to the South. And feeling guilty, had to continue its criticisms of our region to justify itself. So it went. . . . And so it is today.

"The North and South were not a right and wrong cause fighting each other but two bad consciences, each covering up its guilt and its greed, each insisting on its right to sin in its own way, each having economic and religious and psychological reasons for doing so.

"And yet, back of this conflict waged by two bad consciences, was the Negro; back of it, was the terrible need of enslaved human beings to be free; but there were few, North or South, willing to face up to this problem. They were so concerned with themselves, and their hostility toward each other, and their hurt pride and hurt greed, that there was no room left in their minds and hearts for a concern for another group's rights. *Human rights, man's freedom.* . . . Such phrases were as remote as the moon on a blazing hot day to these white men stricken by their hatred for each other.

"Most of our families could not take these traumatic experiences in a sane, creative way. There was too much. And their past life, their values, their beliefs, their mental habits had not prepared them for this kind of trouble.

Insight was not a quality their culture valued; nor intellectual honesty; nor self-criticism; nor concern for human rights; nor could they laugh at themselves. With all their capacity for gaiety and wit, they had so little real humor —it was the backwoodsman who possessed humor and his voice was not heard at this time. All these planter families had was courage and anger, and it was not enough.

"Yet there were individuals, all over the South, who kept themselves without hate, admitting the South's mistakes, and refusing to believe in the tenets of white supremacy. There were others who showed great valor and personal courage in working out family problems, though they were defensive and confused in their thinking about the region. But most gave up, did things the easy way regardless of human consequences, thought the easy way, and identifying with the group, dissolved their scruples by substituting for a personal conscience and a clear brain this thing our politicians call 'loyalty to southern tradition.'

"Event after hard event piled up. The South was in chaos. Many had lost their citizenship, homes, possessions, and were psychological aliens in their own beloved country. And suddenly four million Negroes were 'freed' with nowhere to go, nowhere to sleep, no work, no food, no 'place,' no schools.

"And the Yankee accent was everywhere. Southerners began to hate the sound of it for so rarely did it come from mouths that spoke words of tact or sympathy. But, as miserable as was the whites' condition, and it was bad, the condition of Negroes was worse. It was this problem of rehabilitation of Negroes (the whites were left to shift for themselves) that the Freedmen's Bureau worked on. After all, though Congress found it hard to remember, the war had been fought to 'free the slaves.' The Bureau's blunders were a thing of horror, but at the same time, much that was urgently needed was done and the worst strains were eased. The Bureau found work for Negroes, negotiated labor contracts with white employers, opened schools, and gave them much needed health care. But the white South was too confused to feel relief that part of the region's burden was lifted in this way. Instead they hated these 'carpetbaggers' for their concern for Negroes and their lack of concern for whites. Like a jealous, sick, miserable child, they wanted all the attention and had little pity for those worse off than themselves.

"But there were other northerners, not interested in Negroes, who came also, and stayed long after the Bureau closed up. And southerners worked side by side with them as they set up factories at the level of the South's starvation wages, and in this way, an odd kind of unity was finally established between the two regions. The North furnished the money, the South furnished the labor and the managerial talent and its region's resources, and it worked—as colonial systems always work, for a time.

"It worked for a time because these men, southern and northern, had energy, when most of our families felt paralyzed by trouble. They knew things to do; they went about doing them. They were often—southern and northern—tough and selfish and greedy, but they brought order out of chaos.

"In the rural regions, fewer northerners were seen, but other southerners brought order there and that order was based on the sharecropping system. No one stopped to examine its moral roots or its economic implications. People needed a roof over their heads. They needed corn bread for supper. Whites and Negroes took it when it was offered them. They hungered for peace and a few quiet nights and the knowledge that tomorrow they would have a little to eat, and they were willing to pay any price for these necessities.

"In a way, sharecropping seemed a perfect solution.

There were few jobs available off the farms. Few factories, and few men trained to do anything but farm work, and no money to pay wages with. Confederate money was nothing but paper after Lee surrendered. In our house, when I was a child, there were piles of it in an old trunk upstairs. I remember we children took a basketful downtown to see if it would buy a dime's worth of candy. When the storekeeper said, 'No,' my brother tried to bargain with him. 'Even a trunkful of it?' he said. 'Not even a warehouse full,' the man answered. We were stunned. But our grandfathers had no such illusions. They knew they had nothing but land. So it seemed a good thing to say: 'Now listen, you go back on the farm and get to work. I'll feed you and you can live in one of the cabins. When it's cotton-picking time, I'll pay you a share of what you've raised on my land.' So the system began.

"But once beginning, there was no end to it. It made too much money for a few folks, and too little for the rest for them to buy land of their own, or leave to learn new trades or find new jobs. And it was so easy for the few. You sat in the big house and a hundred, maybe a thousand, colored and white folks raised your crop. Now and then, you put fertilizer on the land if you had the cash to buy it, or if you didn't you let them bleed it to death. You bought the seed, furnished a few mules, sat back and let the 'hands' do the rest. When fall came, you sold the cotton—or the tobacco—gave them their share or a part of it, depending on how honest you were. To feed the workers through the winter, you put up a commissary on your place, charged the colored and white folks high interest on the food you sold them 'on time' and deducted it in September when cotton was picked and weighed up. You, on the other hand, paid high interest at the bank for the money to carry your workers through the winter; you lost your crop when growing conditions were bad; prices were so low some years that you didn't make a cent and when that happened you had to feed the families on your place no matter how hard it was to do; but the good years were good and when they came a few made enormous profits. And these few dug in: buying the farms of their neighbors who were not as shrewd traders in the market as they, growing richer as the years went by, controlling more and more sharecroppers, white and colored, who were as tied to these farms by low wages and long hours and ignorance as if they had been legal slaves.

"That is the way it began.

"My parents grew up in those troubled years and when we were born they tried to give us a better childhood than theirs had been. That meant material things but it meant ideals and values too. They gave us ideals they did not practice and did not expect us to practice and which we could not have practiced had we wanted to. And yet they urged us to believe in them. At the same time we were urged to believe in segregation too and loyalty to southern tradition.

"And that is what you find so hard to understand. And I too have found it hard. We need to remember the chaos, the confusion, the hurt feelings, the poverty. The church, which might have been a guiding principle through this bleak and terrifying time, had made so grave a compromise with Christian belief on the issue of slavery that its leaders, still defensive and guilty, were hardly in a position to give moral guidance. So, a kind of gentleman's agreement came about that a state of emergency existed within the areas of race and money and politics which necessitated a suspension of morals in these fields. Preachers, politicians, judges, planters, factory owners, and plain working folks agreed. People did not confess it aloud. They still talked about sin, and sometimes even about democracy. And as time went on, the less they practiced their ideals the more they cherished them, as if the ideals were something rare that was no longer durable enough for the life everybody had to live yet must be kept safe somewhere, at least in the corner of one's memory, and maybe some day could be lived again.

"Our people were meeting trouble by closing up their lives, minds, hearts, consciences, trying not to see, not to feel things as they really were.

"When your parents and I were children, economic order had in a sense been restored although there was great poverty. But race feeling in the South had reached its peak. The decade before we were born, a thousand Negroes were lynched. The Klan had ridden in almost every county, drawing under its hood the haters and the hotheads from many families. People were terrified not only of Negroes but of their own capacity for cruelty, and panic-stricken at the lack of wise leadership. And in church, not a word was preached about these matters, no insight given that might have restrained excesses, no words said to encourage men and women to try to meet their challenge as Christian citizens living in a democracy.

"I have sometimes thought: had there been a few men in the South with enough strength to be humble and admit their region's mistakes, with enough integrity and energy to act out their own beliefs and with a strong belief in freedom and a clear vision of a new way of life, our people might have been swung around with their faces turned to the future. But we had no leaders of moral and intellectual stature, no one of the quality of a Nehru in India; certainly no one comparable to Gandhi. We had only one Robert E. Lee, and he retired during the troubled times of Reconstruction to a college campus. There was Henry Grady, it is true, the 'conciliator,' who talked a certain kind of good common sense that seemed lucid and statesmanlike in comparison with most, though he showed little awareness of the moral problems of human relations so completely unsolved or the economic and social needs of the eighty per cent of whites who were not in the dominant group.

"But our leaders were, for the most part, hotheaded, uninformed, defensive, greedy men, unwilling to accept criticism. Or else they were so tortured and ambivalent that they found it impossible to make important decisions quickly enough. So the South walked backward into its future. It is no wonder people were hurt on the journey.

"My oldest brother was born the year that the Supreme Court nullified the restrictive features of the Civil Rights Acts. And from then on the South felt that it was free to do what it wished about segregation. The first statutes were so profitable to politician and economic exploiter that more and more statutes were added. It happened so quickly that people did not realize what had been done to their lives.

"When we look back on those years, it seems as if the whole white South suffered a moral breakdown. And yet, we must remember that there were no massive sadistic orgies as in Germany, no gas chambers, concentration camps, no Buchenwald and Dachau. Always the South's conscience hurt; always there were doubts and scruples; always hate was tempered with a little love, and always folks were inconsistent—which was a blessed thing for our region. Ideals seemed to be dead but at least their ghosts haunted men's souls.

"But in those eighty years after the Civil War nearly five thousand human beings *were* lynched. We can't forget that either, for it is a heavy sin for a democratic Christian people to live with. Yet it is different in quantity and quality from the six million Jews killed so quickly in Germany. Different and in a way more evil. For we used those lynchings as a symbolic rite to keep alive in men's minds the idea of white supremacy and we set up a system of avoidance rites that destroyed not bodies but the spirit of men."

"I wonder how the Negroes felt," the girl whispered. "I've never thought about it. But the children, how did it make them feel? I guess it is strange that I've never tried to imagine how they felt."

"I suppose there is no way you can feel it, truly, unless you live through it. We whites have a color glaze on our imaginations that makes it hard to feel with the people we have segregated ourselves from. But I think, as they watched the signs go up, and saw wall after wall built by law to shut them out from the life of their nation, that many of them blocked it off just as did white people. I think maybe they drew a little circle around their small personal lives and tried not to look beyond, for there were sinister sounds and shadows outside. They filled these small lives with work and raising their families and their hope of heaven and a struggle for education, and dancing and razor fights and dreams and laughter. And there was singing, the saddest singing in all the world, and the most beautiful. And sometimes we who caused the sadness would weep with them as they sang."

"The North can't understand that," she interrupted softly, "but I do. And I think it makes us seem a little more decent."

"Maybe it makes us only more complex. But anyway, most adjusted as quietly as possible and tried to make the best of the little they had. Sometimes they have been called Uncle Toms for this and 'handkerchief heads' by people in the North though I think they were only trying to hold on to sanity in a world of madness. And some, having been given an education, began to try to find a rational way out for their people. But a few angry bitter ignorant Negroes did fight back and in the only way they knew how: by assaulting white women. It didn't happen often but it happened and it was a powerful and suicidal revenge. White men had ruthlessly used Negro women

for a hundred and fifty years and carelessly abandoned
their children. It was natural that a few Negro men should
try to hurt the white race in the same way they had
been hurt. But it was like pouring gasoline on a fire. And
every mind in the South was scorched by the heat.

"People said, 'You see? We have to have a lynching
now and then. You see? This is why segregation is right!'

"Your parents and I lived our babyhood in those days
of wrath. But always the violence was distant, the words
vague and terrible for we were protected children. A
lynching could happen in our county and we wouldn't
know it. Yet we did know because of faces, whispers, a
tightening of the whole town."

I did not say more for I was caught in those old days,
remembering: Sometimes it was your nurse who made
you know. You loved her, and suddenly she was frightened, and you knew it. Her eyes saw things your eyes
did not see. As the two of you sat in the sand playing
your baby games, she'd whisper, "Lawd Jesus, when you
going to help us!" And suddenly the play would leave
the game and you would creep close to her begging her
to shield you from her trouble. . . . Sometimes it would
be your father, explaining a race incident to the older
children. Even now I can feel that hush, the changed
voices when they saw you listening, the talking down to
the little one in false and cheerful words, saying, "Sugar,
what you been playing today?"

So we suffered the grown folks' trouble, but without
understanding. Cruel things were learned casually. You
would be in the buggy with your father, out near the
turpentine still where the convict gang worked, as was
done in those days, on your father's turpentine farm. A
foreman would came over and make his report. "What
he needs is the sweat box," sometimes he'd say of a
troublesome Negro. And you'd sit there listening while
chills curled over your body and mind. "No," your father

would reply quietly, "we can't do that. Straighten him out another way." And you were glad your father wouldn't let him do these things, but you had heard the word *sweat box* before you could spell it, and you knew your father's friends did use the sweat box or stocks or whipping as punishment for the convicts leased out to them and these same friends gave you and your little sister candy and dimes and sometimes brought you presents from Savannah. Strange, how you remember a little bag of candy and a sweat box together. . . .

I sat there facing the girl, thinking of the old questions, the fears of childhood. But you shut the bad away and remembered only the pleasant, the games, shadows of clouds moving across sunny grass, sugar cane and boiled peanuts and figs . . . odd wispy things . . . like sticking banana shrubs up your nostrils for the sweet smell of it, or taking a handkerchief full of them to teacher. These are the things white children remembered. It is so easy to see the old scuppernong vine you used to climb in the summer, sitting on top of the trellis eating grapes until tummy was tight and round, watching hens below peck up pulps from the sand and gulp them with a quick turn of the head . . . soft glazey pulp, peck, gulp. . . . It is easy to see this. So hard to see Something swinging from a limb—because you never saw it. You only heard the whispers, saw the horror of it in dark faces you loved. Once I heard the thin cracking shots of a drunken farmer on Saturday, killing a Negro who had sassed him. Sometimes, suddenly, those shots ring through my ears as if it had happened a moment ago. But not often. There is too much that made me love the place where I was born, that makes me even now want to remember only the good things. . . .

The door closes so quietly. But when trouble blows hard, it flies open, fears creep out, bigger now and greedier, having fed on other fears that we shut up with them, when we were babies. People my age have memories like this, that can trample the reason down when there is talk of change or race violence.

"It isn't all greed," I heard myself say aloud, "though some still believe segregation pays."

She looked up quickly as if she too had forgot that we were talking.

"By the time we were as old as you," I continued, "things had quieted down. Race relations seemed 'settled.' Segregation had hardened around our lives and feelings. The newspapers had worked out a system of leaving out everything they thought might 'upset the people.' Many evil things happened down here but few knew about them. And this false peace gave an ease to men's minds. They could almost believe our life was good and right, and they hated anyone who disturbed this feeling.

"So we learned to do what southern tradition told us to do. Though our conscience sometimes hurt, we obeyed the laws. We did not use the word *dictator*, for we thought of ourselves as free Americans, but we obeyed this invisible power as meekly as if Hitler or Stalin had given the orders. We felt we had no other choice."

"But is it never to end?" she said. "It's like a nightmare everybody is having together! I am glad to know how it started but who is going to stop it? Is it going on and on and on?"

"Not if your generation refuses to let it."

"But how can a person like me do anything! No matter how wrong you think it is, laws are against you, custom is against you, your own family is against you. How do you begin? I guess," she said slowly, "if you hated your family, it would be easier to fight for what is right, down here. It would be easier if you didn't care how much you hurt them."

We had made the circle and were beginning that old treadmill route that the tortured southern liberal knows so well. We were tired, it was late. I told her we would talk again another time. I told her there were ways out of the trap, things were changing a little, and people could change anything, even segregation, if they really wanted to. . . . If they really wanted to. . . .

4

The Stolen Future

I HAVE never forgotten that night and the girl's hurt questions, or those children and their little play or the way we fixed its ending to "make it happy," pretending a decency and grace that are against the laws of our region.

It seems such a little thing, doesn't it? A few children gathered on a mountain making a play—a small play to be presented only before their parents—of Every Child living on a planet alone, who tries to reach out and embrace his universe and finds that he cannot because Religion will not show him the way, and Science is too busy with the making of machines and gadgets and bombs to use its resources to help him, and Conscience has learned no new lessons since childhood, and only Southern Tradition is strong and vigilant in acting out its beliefs.

Out of that play came questions asked by a young girl who used a young girl's words, but no wise man of our earth could have asked more important ones.

I had not tried to give her answers. I had tried only to give her understanding of the difficulties of her elders—of all of us who have failed so miserably in the culturing of children. Knowing that bitterness is a poor bent key to use to unlock the future, I wanted her to begin her search for answers with sympathy for those who had not found them. I knew it would be hard enough for her who so passionately loved her ideals and a family that did not share them.

For twenty-five years a procession of children had come to our mountain, stayed a few summers, passed on. Sensitive, intelligent, eager, quick with their questions, generous and honest—fine raw material for the future. And much of it had been wasted by a region that values color more than children.

I sat there that night thinking of those children—sleeping in little cabins under the trees. Though they had been shocked by this dilemma which their play had exposed to their minds, most of them would soon forget. Busy with tennis and swimming and games they would forget that they once wanted to play with all the world's children. And when they returned home it would be almost as easy as ever to live the old segregated life. Though they would live it with as much kindness and grace as possible, they were too intimate a part of it, had been too rarely hurt by it, to fail to adjust to it. They would content themselves with small acts of decency; they would oppose violence and vulgarity; they would want more things "for Negroes" and "for the poor" and would work for these things. But they would not reject the old way of life. Only a few would try to cut the umbilical cord.

These few would be important. Their dreams, faith, belief in love and nonviolence would sustain them as they began the herculean task of pulling down the walls between themselves and their world. They would not be tempted by communism.

But how about that small number of young Southerners who had drawn close to communism—at least in their sympathies? Why had they done so?

I see it this way: They were young idealists who could not believe they had abandoned one iron box only to

crawl into another for safety. One form of totalitarianism they had been born into and had accepted in childhood. They were too close to it to feel its basic similarities
with another totalitarian system. All they could see was
how ugly is the mask of white supremacy. This mask had
the shadow of a dead man swinging across it; it was
lighted up by cross burnings, streaked with the vulgarity
and greed of decades of demagoguery and thievery, of
dishonest state governments, of vast poverty, of men who
sell their integrity for votes, twisted by a cruel disregard
for the growth of the human spirit.

With memory full of such evils and their spirit revolt-
ing against them, the vague evils of the political system of
Russia seemed far away. They could not realize in their
imagination a country they had never visited, a vast,
tumultuous revolution that had taken place before they
were born and of which they had only hearsay reports.
They had read of the millions in slave camps, of the firing
line for leaders who deviated from the official party
opinion, of the heavy suspicion under which even loyal
Communists lived. Stories such as these were for them in
the shadowland between fantasy and fact. Years of reading headlines and comic books, of seeing violence in
movies, of listening to their own demagogues blow up
big lies from small truths, had developed in them a
resistance to believing anything which they had not come
in actual contact with.

But they had come in contact with evils in their own
region which were accepted and defended by southern
political and church leaders, all of whom claimed to be
"democratic Americans"—many of whom were on a
witch hunt not only to find "Communists" but to find
every honest liberal in the South.

Sheer disgust at the hypocrisy and racism of these
Congressmen drove a few young Southerners toward
communism. They took their own freedom for granted.

They could not conceive of its being withdrawn from them by any power on earth. At the same time, they resented being made to do wrong in the South: compelled by law to go through doors marked *White*, compelled by law to sit in the front of buses even though shamed by this silly symbol of arrogance. They were not proud of their parents who kept silent about segregation. They were young enough to feel change sweeping across the earth and they wanted heroism to march forth gallantly to meet it. But there was little heroism among the nice people they knew. They had read of the underground in Europe, of young people who worked together in what seemed to be a warm camaraderie for goals that seemed good and right and who, tortured for their beliefs, had proudly died for them. These young southerners ached to risk something big for something good but they knew among their own people they would be called only fools.

It was not that they had more love for their fellowmen than had liberal non-Communists. Perhaps they had only more impatience. Perhaps because they had resented the "unfairnesses" of their own childhood they could identify more easily with unfair treatment of strangers. Whatever the names of the little seeds that fell in childhood soil, they sprouted into a sympathy for all men in trouble and an impatience with hypocrisy and inaction. It was a tragic thing to watch these young southerners move with so much valor from one little stage to another on which authority would once more play out its old drama and to know that they did so because in the strongest democracy on earth they were not free to live their ideals.

I have in front of me, as I write, a sheaf of clippings: words said by white men of the South. And as I turn these pages reading what the South's leaders have said I cannot forget all the South's children who have listened:

. . . But we will resist to the bitter end, whatever the consequences, any measure or any movement which would have a tendency to bring about social equality and intermingling and amalgamation of the races in our states.

—Senator Richard Russell,
during FEPC filibuster, 1946

. . . I would say to the Negro: before demanding to be a white man socially and politically, learn to be a white man morally and intellectually—and to the white man: the black man is our brother, a younger brother, not adult, not disciplined, but tragic, pitiable, and lovable; act as his brother and be patient.

—William Alexander Percy,
Lanterns on the Levee, 1941

Only a fool would say the Southern pattern of separation of the races can, or should be overthrown.

—*Atlanta Constitution*,
Editorial, Sept. 26, 1948

The yellow people, the brown people and the blacks are mentally unfit for directors in our form of government. You can not change these natural and God-ordained mental processes. . . . When, and if, our voters' list contains a large percentage of voters of other than Caucasian stock, then our constitutional form of government becomes impossible and unworkable. . . . No educational test will discern this natural difference in voters.

—Tom Linder, Georgia Commissioner of Agriculture,
in a letter to the *Atlanta Journal*, 1948

The permanent betterment of race relations cannot be brought about unless the ground is cleared by recognition on the part of both races that the problem will not yield to a cure-all solution, and that the explosive issue of segregation must not be called into question.

—David L. Cohn,
Where I was Born and Raised, 1948

The way to control the nigger is to whip him when he does not obey without it, and another is never to pay him more wages than is actually necessary to buy food and clothing.

—W. K. Vardaman, quoted by
W. J. Cash, *Mind of the South*

Whenever the Constitution [of the United States] comes between me and the virtue of the white women of the South, I say to hell with the Constitution!

—Cole Blease, quoted by
W. J. Cash, *Mind of the South*

The Negro, not having assimilated the white man's ethics, giving only lip service to the white man's morality, must for his own peace and security accept whole-heartedly the white man's mores and taboos.

—William Alexander Percy,
Lanterns on the Levee, 1941

I cannot emphasize one point too strongly. The white South is as united as 30,000,000 people can be in its insistence upon segregation. Federal action cannot change them. It will be tragic for the South, the Negro, and the nation itself if the government should enact and attempt to enforce any laws or Supreme Court decisions that would open the South's public schools and public gathering places to the Negro.

—Hodding Carter,
Atlanta Journal, Sept. 3, 1948

Political equality means social equality and social equality means intermarriage, and that means the mongrelizing of the American race. . . . I cannot and will not be a party to the recognition of the Fourteenth and Fifteenth Amendments.

–Ellison D. Smith,
U.S. Congress, 1932

Why can words such as these, which our politicians use whenever the issue of civil rights comes up, stir such deep anxiety in men's hearts? How can one idea like segregation become so hypnotic a thing that it binds a whole people together, good, bad, strong, weak, ignorant and learned, sensitive, obtuse, psychotic and sane, making them one as only a common worship or a deeply shared fear can do? Why has the word taken on the terrors of taboo and the sanctity of religion? What makes it so important to us that men will keep themselves poor to sustain it, out of jobs to defend it? Why is it so sacred that the church has let it eat the heart out of religion? Why will not Christian ministers in the South—with the exception of a valiant handful—preach against it? Why is it that newspaper editors will not write editorials opposing it? The answer surely is worth searching for.

When taxicab drivers, and store owners, bankers, farmers, Christian ministers, doctors, politicians, patients in mental hospitals and their attendants, writers, university presidents, union members and mill owners, newspaper editors, garbage collectors and Rotarians, rich and poor, men and women, unite in common worship and common fear of one idea we know it has come to hold deep and secret meanings for each of them, as different as are the people themselves. We know it has woven itself around fantasies at levels difficult for the mind to touch, until it is a part of each man's internal defense system, embedded like steel in his psychic fortifications. And, like the little dirty rag or doll that an unhappy child sleeps with, it has acquired inflated values that extend far beyond the rational concerns of economics and government, or the obvious profits and losses accruing from the white-supremacy system, into childhood memories long repressed.

Why is this so?

Why, said the girl, *does Daddy want to keep Negroes segregated—what pleasure does he get out of it? Does it make him richer to keep them that way?* . . .

Do you think we should break laws? she said. . . .

If they've made up their mind that the signs stay up and segregation is going to be here forever then why do they fool themselves? Why pretend and go to church and say nice words? It doesn't make sense. . . .

Since we have to practice segregation why didn't you make us believe it is right? When I have children I am not going to give them a single ideal they can't practice. . . .

If you hated your family it would be easier to fight for what is right down here. . . .

You cannot forget words like this if you have ever heard a young voice say them.

Part Two

The White Man's Burden

1

The Lessons

IT BEGAN so long ago, not only in the history books but in our childhood. We southerners learned our first three lessons too well.

I do not think our mothers were aware that they were teaching us lessons. It was as if they were revolving mirrors reflecting life outside the home, inside their memory, outside the home, and we were spectators entranced by the bright and terrible images we saw there. The mirror might be luminous or streaked, or so dimmed that reflections were no more than shadows, but we learned from this preview of the world we were born into, what was expected of us as human creatures.

We were taught in this way to love God, to love our white skin, and to believe in the sanctity of both. We learned at the same time to fear God and to think of Him as having complete power over our lives. As we were beginning to feel this power and to see it reflected in our parents, we were learning also to fear a power that was in our body, and to fear dark people who were everywhere around us, though the ones who came into our homes we were taught to love.

By the time we were five years old we had learned, without hearing the words, that masturbation is wrong and segregation is right, and each had become a dread taboo that must never be broken, for we believed God, whom we feared and tried desperately to love, had made the rules concerning not only Him and our parents, but our bodies and Negroes. Therefore when we as small children crept over the race line and ate and played with Negroes or broke other segregation customs known to us, we felt the same dread fear of consequences, the same overwhelming guilt we felt when we crept over the sex line and played with our body, or thought thoughts about God or our parents that we knew we must not think. Each was a "sin," each "deserved punishment," each would receive it in this world or the next. Each was tied up with the other and all were tied close to God.

These were our first lessons. Wrapped together, they were taught us by our mother's voice, memorized with her love, patted into our lives as she rocked us to sleep or fed us. As the years passed, we learned other lessons and discovered interesting ways of cheating on them but these first rules of our life were sacred. They were taboos which we dared not break. Yet we did break them, for it was impossible to observe them. We broke the rules and told ourselves we had kept them. We were not liars; we were human, and only used the ways the human mind has of meeting an insoluble problem. We believed certain acts were so wrong that they must never be committed and then we committed them and denied to ourselves that we had done so. It worked very well. Our minds had split: hardly more than a crack at first, but we began in those early years a two-leveled existence which we have since managed quite smoothly.

The acts which we later learned were "bad" never seemed really "bad" to us; at least we could find excuses for them. But those we learned were "bad" before we were five years old were CRIMES that we could not excuse; we could only forget. Though many a southerner has

lived a tough hardened life since the days his mother
rocked him until his eyes were glazed with sleep, his
anxiety is, even now, concerned largely with the moral
junk pile which he wandered around in when a little
child. But more important perhaps than the ethical
residue left in our minds was the process of this learning
which gave our emotions their Gothic curves.

Our first lesson about God made the deepest impression
on us. We were told that He loved us, and then we were
told that He would burn us in everlasting flames of hell
if we displeased Him. We were told we should love Him
for He gives us everything good that we have, and then
we were told we should fear Him because He has the
power to do evil to us whenever He cares to. We learned
from this part of the lesson another: that "people," like
God and parents, can love you and hate you at the same
time; and though they may love you, if you displease
them they may do you great injury; hence being loved
by them does not give you protection from being harmed
by them. We learned that They (parents) have a "right"
to act in this way because God does, and that They in a
sense represent God, in the family.

Sometimes, when we felt weakened by anxieties that
we had no words for, and battered by impulses impossible
to act out, we tried to believe that God was responsible
for this miserable state of affairs and one should not be
too angry with parents. At least we thought this as we
grew older and it helped some of us make a far more
harmonious adjustment to our parents than to God.

As the years passed, God became the mighty protag-
onist of ambivalence although we had not heard the word.
He loomed before us as the awesome example of one who
injures, even destroys, in the name of "good" those whom
He loves, and does it because He has the "right" to. We
tried to think of Him as our best friend because we were

told that He was. Weak with fear, we told ourselves that when you break the rules you "should be punished" by Him or your parents. But a doubt, an earthy animal shrewdness, whispered that anyone who would harm us was also our enemy. Yet these whispers we dared not say aloud, or clearly to ourselves, for we feared we might drop dead if we did. Even a wispy thought or two loaded us down with unbearable guilt. As we grew older and began to value reason and knowledge and compassion, we were told that He was wise and all-loving; yet He seemed from Old Testament stories to be full of whimsies and terrifying impulses and definitely not One whom a child could talk to and expect to receive an understanding reply from.

He was Authority. And we bowed before His power with that pinched quietness of children, stoically resigning ourselves to this Force as it was interpreted by the grown folks.

But life seemed a lost battle to many of us only after we learned the lesson on the Unpardonable Sin. Then it was that man's fate, our fate certainly, was sealed. According to this lesson, received mainly at revival meetings but graven on our hearts by our parents' refusal to deny it, God forgave, if we prayed hard and piteously enough, all sins but one. This one sin "against the Holy Ghost" He would never forgive. Committing it, one lived forever among the damned. What this sin was, what the "Holy Ghost" was, no one seemed to know. Or perhaps even grown folks dared not say it aloud. But the implication was—and this was made plain—that if you did not tread softly you would commit it; the best way was never to question anything but always accept what you were told.

Love and punishment . . . redemption and the unpardonable sin. . . . He who would not harm a sparrow would burn little children in everlasting flames. . . . It added up to a terrible poetry and we learned each line by heart.

[Our second lesson had to do with the body.] A complicated and bewildering lesson—taught us as was our theology, in little slivers and by the unfinished sentence method. But we learned it as we learned all the rest, knowing they were important because of the anxious tones in which they were taught. This lesson, translated into words, went something like this:

"God has given you a body which you must keep clean and healthy by taking baths, eating food, exercising, and having daily elimination. It is good also to take pride in developing skills such as baseball and swimming and fighting, and natural to think a little about the clothes you wear. But the body itself is a Thing of Shame and you must never show its nakedness to anyone except to the doctor when you are sick. Indeed, you should not look at it much yourself, especially in mirrors. It is true that in a sense your body is 'yours' but it isn't yours to feel at home with. It is God's holy temple and must never be desecrated by pleasures—except the few properly introduced to you—though pain, however repulsive, you must accept as having a right to enter this temple as one accepts visits from disagreeable relatives.

"Now, parts of your body are segregated areas which you must stay away from and keep others away from. These areas you touch only when necessary. In other words, you cannot associate freely with them any more than you can associate freely with colored children.

"Especially must you be careful about what enters your body. Many things are prohibited. Among these, probably the easiest to talk about is alcohol. 'Drinking' is a symbol of an evil that begins so early in life that it may be 'inherited,' for one who 'drinks' moves almost from milk bottle to whisky bottle, from the shaky legs of a child to the shaky legs of a drunk. The word *prohibition* means a movement to prohibit strong drink but every one knows that stronger temptations are prohibited with it, just as one knows that *segregation* also shuts one away from irresistible evils. Indeed, prohibition and segregation have much to do with each other, for there are the same mysterious reasons for both of these restrictions. Food, however, is not restricted; you may eat it with a clear conscience and whenever you are hungry.

"As you are beginning to see, what enters and leaves the doors of your body is the essence of morality. Yet if you are a little girl, you should not be aware that there are certain doors. So this question of where babies come from turns into a complicated matter since it concerns both a private entrance and a semi-public exit which each human being has to make but no one wants to remember. It is true that girls are quite involved in this since most of them will some day be mothers but it is better just now for you (whether boy or girl) to accept the idea that storks bring babies, or if you prefer, that they are found in the doctor's bag. At least accept it until you are grown and can face up to the ugliness of the whole business of creation. (I have at moments wondered if moralists had only morals at heart or if they had also the self-esteem of little males in mind when they hid from children the facts of life, fearing perhaps that little females might over-value their role in this drama of creation and, turning 'uppity' as we say in Dixie, forget their inferior place in the scheme of things.)

"The truth of the matter is: the world is full of secrets and the most important are concerned with you and the feelings that roam around in you. The better part of valor is to accept these secrets and never try to find out what they are. Simply remember that morality is based on this mysterious matter of entrances and exits, and Sin hovers over all doors. Also, the Authorities are watching.

"Now, on the other hand, though your body is a thing of shame and mystery, and curiosity about it is not good, your skin is your glory and the source of your strength and pride. It is white. And, as you have heard, whiteness is a symbol of purity and excellence. Remember this: Your white skin proves that you are better than all other people on this earth. Yes, it does that. And does it simply because it is white—which, in a way, is a kind of miracle. But the Bible is full of miracles and it should not be too difficult for us to accept one more." (Southern children did not learn until years later that no one had thought much about skin color until three or four centuries ago when white folks set out from Europe to explore the earth. Nor did they know until they were grown that men in Europe and America had written books about it and a racial philosophy had developed from it which "proved" this Ptolemaic regress in which the white man was the center of the universe and all other races revolved around him in concentric circles. The racists "proved" the white man's superiority, especially the white Christian's, just as Ptolemy long before them had proved that the earth was the center of the universe, and as the theologians of the Middle Ages proved that angels danced on the point of needles, and as Communists prove their fascinating theories that the world and all within it revolve around Marxist economics.)

"Since this is so," our lesson continued, "your skin color is a Badge of Innocence which you can wear as vaingloriously as you please because God gave it to you and hence it is good and right. It gives you priorities over colored people everywhere in the world, and especially those in the South, in matters of where you sit and stand, what part of town you live in, where you eat, the theaters you go to, the swimming pools you use, jobs, the people you love, and so on. But these matters you will learn more about as you grow older."

Exaggerated? Perhaps. Whenever one puts a belief, a way of life, into quick words of course one exaggerates. Distortion, condensation, displacement are used not only by artists and dreamers; they are used every time we speak aloud. Yet when we thought about it at all we southerners came close, in our thinking, to what I have put down here.

This process of learning was as different for each child as were his parents' vocabulary and emotional needs. We cannot wisely forget this. And we learned far more from acts than words, more from a raised eyebrow, a joke, a shocked voice, a withdrawing movement of the body, a long silence, than from long sentences. But however skillfully our grown-up minds have found euphemisms to cover brutalities and gaucheries, however widely we now separate in our memory one lesson from another to avoid their chilling implications, we accepted with scarcely a differing shade of emphasis the lesson outlines sketched here.

The lesson on segregation was only a logical extension of the lessons on sex and white superiority and God. Not only Negroes but everything dark, dangerous, evil must be pushed to the rim of one's life. Signs put over doors in the world outside and over minds seemed natural enough to children like us, for signs had already been put over forbidden areas of our body. The banning of people and books and ideas did not appear more shocking than the banning of our wishes which we learned early to send to the Dark-town of our unconscious. But we clung to the belief, as an unhappy child treasures a beloved toy, that our white skin made us "better" than all other people. And this belief comforted us, for we felt worthless and weak when confronted by Authorities who had cheapened nearly all that we held dear, except our skin color. There, in the Land of Epidermis, every one of us was a little king.

Each lesson was linked on to the other, drawing strength from it. Indeed, the relentless interlocking of these learnings grows more and more clear as one retraces the paths and bypaths circling through a southern childhood. Forbidden play . . . forbidden dreams . . . forbidden relations . . . restlessness . . . resentment . . . guilt . . . emptiness. . . . *Ah there they are! The colored kids. Come on, you all, let's push 'em off the sidewalk. Chocolate drop chocolate drop chocolate drop.* . . . And the answering cry, *Yan yan yan crackers crackers yan yan yan.* . . . Struggle. Sudden strange struggle. Hot feelings pouring over you, driving you to push hard against wiry dark quickbreathing little bodies, push hard until they are off the sidewalk, off into sandspurs and dirt, sobbing angrily, *We'll get even with you you just wait we'll get.* . . . And your crowd, flushed and dazed, walk on, victors for a wan moment over something, you never know what. For you like the colored kids. You don't really mind their walking on the sidewalk. What is a sidewalk! Yet you had to do something and this thing, you knew, THEY WHO MAKE THE RULES would let you do. Though your own mother might scold you for fighting and pushing, if she knew, though your parents might say, "You cannot hurt their feelings, remember that! You must never push any one, no matter who it is," though *your* parents might not approve, yet OTHER PARENTS seem to think pushing little Negroes into sandspurs funny, like tying tin cans to a dog's tail, and THEY WHO MAKE THE RULES seem not to mind at all.

Anyway, this pushing off the sidewalk is not one of the Sins you have to worry about. You somehow know this. Even if Mother doesn't approve, you know it isn't one of the Sins. You do not have to pray about it, for it has never been mentioned in church or Sunday school. You know you will not go to hell if you push little colored kids into sandspurs (or later out of jobs) though you may go there if you steal a nickel or do "bad" things or even think them. Now, if you were to go to church or to school with colored children, that would be worse than a sin, worse than anything you know of. You've learned that somewhere. But how could you do it anyway, for churches and schools would not let the colored kids in even if you would. . . . And then you grow confused and stop thinking and try never again, as long as you live, to think. But you have learned now to know a real sin from a mistake because of the look on faces when THEY talk to you about these matters. It is a secret, shamed look that creeps into their eyes as if THEY too have done naughty things and faces grow tight and worried. Sometimes all grown-up faces look worried as if something is going to happen that even THEY cannot keep from happening. As you lie awake at night thinking about it, you wonder why you never heard anyone talk calmly and pleasantly about the body or race, why no one has ever explained these interesting matters to you. Both are mysteries. Both have to do with Sin. And punishment for sin is inexorable.

This terrifying sense of impending disaster hung over most of us. Here and there a few escaped it in homes of rare sophistication or rare rebellion. And often the favored child of a family was wrapped so securely in a sense of being cherished that the Danger seemed for him remote. But favored children of a home and homes favored by exceptional knowledge and good will could not escape the weight of taboo. It was, for them, padded with love and esteem and a regard for the amenities of the human spirit, and fell more gently on minds and hearts. But once under it, these children too were squeezed by its weight, shaped by it as were all until they, like the rest, became little crooked wedges that fit into the intricately twisting serrated design of life which THEY WHO MAKE THE RULES had prepared for us in Dixie.

Our mothers and fathers would have weakened, I think, had not religion and southern tradition kept them hard at the teaching. Even so, their hearts and their sense of humor gave us many a holiday. There were times when we were not southerner or sinner but just children playing and, like children everywhere, concerned only with making the whole world into a fine toy for our games.

Our parents did more. Their love and pity overwhelmed them, sometimes, after too many strict lessons (which they did not quite believe in), and they guiltily made it up to us, or to themselves, by indulging us in a startling fashion. Poor and rich parents did this. We were petted children, not puritans. Sugar-tit words and sugar-tit experiences too often made of our minds and manners a fatty tissue that hid the sharp rickety bones of our souls. *Honey, sugar, sweetie* were milk names that still cling to our middle-aged vocabulary. Kisses and big hugs, and soothing laps to nuzzle up in, and tea cakes and bread 'n' butter 'n' sugar, and cane syrup poured on hot buttered biscuit, and homemade ice cream and praise, gave a velvety texture to childhood which did not keep out the sharp stabs from the lessons but soften them now in our memory until we deny that we felt them at all. The air was so warm and melting . . . and piles of moss made such thick feathery play houses to romp on under oak trees . . . the stars were close in the night sky and everywhere the sweet smell of flowers . . . how can one dig down deep enough into such a childhood to find the sharp needling lessons that sometimes gave a death-prick to our souls!

Footnotes spring up like weeds in my mind as I write this. For always I remember the next-door neighbor who was different, the friend down the street, or a relative, who was as frugal with pet names and desserts and caresses as with money. The South has its share of tight-lipped, tight-hearted people who rigorously followed a tight little road map on the journey via Dixie to heaven and did not let either their love or their guilt buy indulgences for their children. Like Calvin, from whom so many of our southern precepts came, they bent every little wire in childhood and pinched it to a predestined shape. Nothing was too small to be the concern of these moralists. And yet sometimes their insistence on a frugal diet and frugal clothes and frugal pleasures and frugal use of money and frugal fantasies served as a pruning knife which, as in New England, brought forth a heavy crop of scholarship or missionary zeal.

And there were the families, like my own, whose lives were firmly triangulated on sin, sex, and segregation but who nonetheless were shown a way to become free again. A poor way, perhaps—a giving of artificial legs to a child whose legs have been cut off—yet it helped us walk.

Our mother and nurse and grandmothers petted us. We were sugar-tit children who were given a deep and terrifying anxiety about sin as we were being coddled and comforted. And outside our home we moved in the rigid patterns of segregation that all white southerners live. But our father never stopped saying, and because he believed it, we also believed: that nothing is really important about a man except his being human; that no one should sink so low as to have an enemy; and that work is not only something we owe in payment to an earth that has given us so much, it is also fun.

Such flashes of sanity are not to be treated lightly either in a home or in a region. I know these beliefs are touched with paternalism and middle-class *oblige*. And I am aware also that they who think systems can be better than the people in the system would sneer at grace and good will. That an individual might try in his own personal life to pay back his obligation to past generations who have bestowed so much upon him seems only a romantic gesture to those who think change is brought about by new systems, not by the quality of human growth. Nonetheless, these three beliefs—in work owed to one's earth, in the destructiveness of hate, and in the value of the individual—were like yeast in soggy dough in my family. And there were families throughout the South, more than we have guessed perhaps, who were taught these extracurricular activities of the human spirit.

But when we stepped outside our homes, Custom and Church took charge of our education.

Every little southern town is a fine stage-set for Southern Tradition to use as it teaches its children the twisting turning dance of segregation. Few words are needed for there are signs everywhere. *White . . . colored . . . white . . . colored . . .* over doors of railroad and bus stations, over doors of public toilets, over doors of theaters, over drinking fountains. Sometimes when a town could afford but one drinking fountain, the word *White* was painted on one side of it and *colored* on the other. I have seen that. It means there are a few men in that town whose memories are aching, who want to play fair, and under "the system" can think of no better way to do it. But in most towns with one fountain, only the word *White* is painted on it. The town's white idiot can drink out of it but the town's black college professor must go thirsty on a hot August day.

There are the signs without words: big white church on Main Street, little unpainted colored church on the rim of town; big white school, little ramshackly colored school; big white house, little unpainted cabins; white graveyard with marble shafts, colored graveyard with mounds of dirt. And there are the invisible lines that turn and bend and cut the town into segments. Invisible, but electrically charged with taboo. Places you go. Places you don't go. White town, colored town; white streets, colored streets; front door, back door. Places you sit.

Places you cannot sit.

From the time little southern children take their first step they learn their ritual, for Southern Tradition leads them through its intricate movements. And some, if their faces are dark, learn to bend, hat in hand; and others, if their faces are white, learn to hold their heads high. Some step off the sidewalk while other pass by in arrogance. Bending, shoving, genuflecting, ignoring, stepping off, demanding, giving in, avoiding. . . . Children, moving through the labyrinth made by grownups' greed and guilt and fear.

So we learned the dance that cripples the human spirit, step by step by step, we who were white and we who were colored, day by day, hour by hour, year by year until the movements were reflexes and made for the rest of our life without thinking. Alas, for many white children, they were movements made for the rest of their lives without feeling. What white southerner of my generation ever stops to think consciously where to go or asks himself if it is right for him to go there! His muscles know where he can go and take him to the front of the streetcar, to the front of the bus, to the big school, to the hospital, to the library, to hotel and restaurant and picture show, into the best that his town has to offer its citizens. These ceremonials in honor of white supremacy, performed from babyhood, slip from the conscious mind down deep into muscles and glands and become difficult to tear out.

Southern Tradition taught well: we learned our way of life by doing. You never considered arguing with teacher, because you could not see her. You only felt the iron grip of her hand and knew you must go where all the other children were going. And you learned never, never, to get out of step, for this was a precision dance which you must do with deadly accuracy.

And as you went there were a few words, not many, that you never heard perhaps in your home but they became a chanting that accompanied this strange dance and vibrated with its movements: *Nigger, darkie, never call one mister, never call one mister, but would you want your sister, your sister, 300 years from savagery, states' rights states' rights, invading the home, danger our women our women.* Words that made no sense but beat like jungle drums on nerve endings. White words, that the drum-beaters never let die into silence. There were black words, too: *Yassir boss, yassir boss, howdy mistis, howdy,* words spoken loud and bendingly. *Now ain' dat right, yes mam!* followed by sleazy laughter that turned human dignity into a limp thing. But you liked it. And you felt big, important, superior even, as you heard it, though you might not be able to read or write. There were other words you did not hear and yet somehow you knew they were said: *Lord God that white man. Now don' he think he's somepin! Crackers. Stinking white crackers! Mind your manners but don't trust a one of 'em, hear! Mind your manners, child, or you won't live to be grown. Jesus, how I hate white folks, how I hate them!* Words that would have caused a colored man to die had he said them in the wrong place and yet you knew he said them.

These things you knew as you knew your own name. But Southern Tradition did not think it enough. One day, sometime during your childhood or adolescence, a Negro was lynched in your county or the one next to yours. A human being was burned or hanged from a tree and you knew it had happened. But no one publicly condemned it and always the murderers went free. And afterward, maybe weeks or months or years afterward, you sat casually in the drugstore with one of those murderers and drank the Coke he casually paid for. A "nice white girl" could do that but she would have been run out of town or perhaps killed had she drunk a Coke with the young Negro doctor who was devoting his life in service to his people.

So Southern Tradition taught her bleak routines with flashes of lightning to quicken our steps.

2

Trembling Earth

WE CANNOT understand the church's role as a teacher of southern children without realizing the strength of religion in the lives of everybody, rich and poor. Whether we lived in a big house on College Street, a cottage on the side street or a shanty in mill town, most of us loved church. Sunday was a fiesta, a time for our prettiest dresses, the only day of the week when we wore hats, the only time in summer when little boys slicked back their hair and put on their shoes. And the only day when the church bells rang, Baptist and Methodist, clashing their sounds together in friendly proselyting.

I do not remember that we felt a profound reverence for the Unknown when we entered our church, or that our hearts stretched to touch something bigger than the mind can find words for. I am afraid we were too busy looking at each other's clothes or watching the veins swell out on old Mr. Amster's neck as he sang the Gloria, or staring at little Mr. Pusey as he led the tenors through the vagaries of the anthem.

Church was our town—come together not to kneel in worship but to see each other. God was our Host, we were guests in His House, the altar flowers were fresh and fragrant, and if it was Communion Day the cloth was starched and white and the silver cup out of which every one drank was shining. And though we willingly listened to the sermon if it was not too long, and felt a deep flowing sense of togetherness when we sang the Doxology, we were there also to mend the little broken places in our knowledge of each other.

To children, church was more interesting than school, for the grown folks were there and one's eyes could not get enough of their movements, their quick glances, the sudden stiff droop of those who fell asleep under the minister's soothing words. We liked to be with them. But we liked best of all, classes at Sunday school where we said the golden text and emptied our mite boxes and repeated the stories of Daniel in the lion's den and David and his slingshot.

After church, there would be a good dinner at home, and always guests could be invited.

It was a day set aside, made special, with no empty moment in it. Sunday school, morning worship, junior choir practice, and a walk in the woods to pick violets.

In a few homes, like my own, it was also a time when your father heard you name the books of the Bible, or listened encouragingly as you repeated ten Psalms from memory, or asked you odd questions about the old Prophets and tripped you flat with verses whose source you must identify. But we liked the old mouth-filling names, the strange adventures which the Israelites had, and the indignant invectives so eloquently hurled by the prophets at the weak ones on that long troubled journey that seemed never to end but went on from Sunday to Sunday.

The revival meetings in August were different.

The church's emphasis on revival meetings and the revival's effect upon southern personality are difficult to understand unless we let our minds fill with echoes of distance and darkness and ignorance and violence and worn-out bodies and land. For all are tied up with each other and have much to do with the quality of the southern conscience that is stretched so tightly on its frame of sin and punishment and God's anger.

Belief in Some One's right to punish you is the fate of all children in Judaic-Christian culture. But nowhere else, perhaps, have the rich seedbeds of Western homes found such a growing climate for guilt as is produced in the South by the combination of a warm moist evangelism and racial segregation. This flowering of revivals, conversions, deathbed repentance, mourners' bench, love feasts, and fundamentalism must be credited in part also to the historical circumstance of the Brothers John and Charles Wesley's and George Whitfield's visits to Georgia. We can hardly overestimate the influence of these three preachers of God on the mind of the South, for they were men of powerful personality, burning with a powerful belief in the importance of the common man's uncommon soul, and a powerful talent for making men believe in their soul's sacredness by giving size to their sins. It was a curious inversion, this proving a man's stature by the great black shadow he cast, but it worked. Men believed in their importance by believing in the importance of their sins and grew a pride in possessing a conscience that persecuted them.

These young giants of Methodism—not long out of Oxford and full of their discovery of the poor man's soul—came to the New World with their new way of preaching that was intimate and direct and deeply sincere. They went straight to the anxiety in the minds of these tough settlers and whipped up a froth that obliterated rational processes, then released them by showing them a clear narrow road to salvation. Circuit riders who followed them for more than a century continued this emphasis on the rebirth of the soul, as they moved from settlement to settlement preaching the Gospel. They were brave, tireless, passionate men who traveled on horseback, like old Peter Cartwright, three hundred miles a week, preaching four or five times a week, sometimes two or three times a day. Devoted to God and terrified of Him, they made Him into the Despot the people had left behind them when they fled Europe; and by threats of hell, they turned the rebels once more into meek lambs. They did far more than this of course, for men *were* reborn; they did, as it were, re-enter their mother's womb, and many of them found a peace that was real and a way of life that added kindness and decency to a South that had too little of either.

The loneliness, ignorance, and isolation of the rural South made these old preachers welcome everywhere. In spite of their lashing sermons—perhaps because of them —wherever they went, the crossroads saloonkeeper vied with pillars of the church for the privilege of putting them up for the night, for all were hungry for news of a world they were completely cut off from, and fascinated by the power of men who believed and lived their belief.

They were brave men, these circuit riders, who could kill a rattler or swamp panther or wild turkey with casual accuracy or throw a drunken bully out of their meeting with no more than a comma's pause in their sermon. They were veterans pioneering for God, taking danger and death as quietly as they took their sleep. When they spoke, men listened. They preached on the sins that tough frontiersmen committed: drinking, fighting to kill, fornication, self-abuse, gambling, and stealing. And because they made these sins of heroic size by a passionate eloquence that modern preachers cannot equal, no other sins have ever seemed real to the southern imagination but become merely vexatious problems that do not belong in church. They preached, at times, of Jesus and his love, and turned their brush-arbor congregation into wistful blubbering children who, there in the lonely woods, wept for something lost that they knew they could never find again on this earth but hoped to find in heaven.

Such men there were in both Methodist and Baptist churches (whose combined membership is about eighty per cent of the South's churchgoing people)—eloquent, fiery, compelling—and for more than a century they shaped and gave content to the conscience of southerners, rich and poor.

Camp meetings and revivals are the South's past, and once were a heroic part of that past. Today, though often cheapened and vulgarized to the point of obscenity, they are still part of the South's present. Guilt was then and is today the biggest crop raised in Dixie, harvested each summer just before cotton is picked. No wonder that God and Negroes and Jesus and sin and salvation were baled up together in southern children's minds and in many an old textile magnate's also.

When I was a child the annual revivals were a source of enormous terror and at the same time a blessed respite from monotony. Nothing but a lynching or a political race-hate campaign could tear a town's composure into as many dirty little rags or give as many curious satisfactions. Like political demagogues, the evangelists enjoyed people. And, like them, they won allegiance by bruising and then healing a deep fear within men's minds. They loved God too, but they feared Him far more than they loved Him and they urgently wanted their fellowmen to be saved from His wrath. They believed their way of salvation was "right," as did the old circuit riders, and could not conceive of another way of avoiding destruction. And their faith released an enormous energy which in most of us is locked tight in a struggle between the two halves of our nature.

They preached asceticism but preached it with the libertine's words. And, as they preached, they looked as unlike an ascetic as you can imagine. These were potent men —anyone is wrong to think otherwise—who used their potency in their ardent battle for souls.

How can such men be called hypocrites, as they are grossly represented by most novels and plays written about them? They have had numerous counterfeit followers who were—mean nasty tight men who today wander up and down Tobacco Road in Dixie and Tobacco Road in Detroit spreading their gospel of fear and hate; men who preach more against the evils of communism than the evils of sex but are concerned almost wholly with these two "sins." These are the rotted culls of an evangelism that once was a respected and important part of protestant religion.

The revivalists I knew as a child lived their religion and lived it honestly. It is true they were ambivalent men who had healed themselves by walling off one segment of their life and who kept many doors open in their personality by keeping one door securely locked. And they were men whose powerful instincts of sex and hate were woven together into a sadism that would have devastated their lives and broken their minds had they acknowledged it for what it was. Instead, they bound it into verbal energy and with this power of the tongue they drove men in herds toward heaven, lashing out at them cruelly when they seemed to be stampeding, persuading them with laughter and tears when they moved in the right direction but too slowly. And in doing this, they felt they were doing God's will. They were saving souls and they believed any method was justified, if by using it, they could say, "Here, Lord, is one more for Thy Kingdom."

They were sincere if ham actors—a few of them almost touched greatness now and then—and they brought to a South bereft of entertainment and pleasure a brief sur-

cease from the gnawing monotony that ate our small-town
lives away. They often presented this entertainment with
style and always with drama, for they were unafraid to
explore the forbidden places of man's heart. There are
few artists today who would dare probe so ruthlessly the
raw sores of our life as did these evangelists. They were
not wise men but they were shrewd in the use of mass
psychology. They were curiously indifferent to cultural
patterns or else in violent loyalty defended the barbed
wires crisscrossing our age on which their own lives had
been wounded. And they could turn into stupid foolish
men when confronted with questions that ask "Why?"
Wherever their answers came from, that place did not
send them answers to the problems of poverty, of race
segregation, unions, wages, illness and ignorance, war,
and waste of forest and soil and human relations, or answers to the old question of human freedom which
swings around and around in the currents of change
until its light blinds men with fury and drives them to
build institutions or police states to shut out its shining.

Their religion was too narcistic to be concerned with
anything but a man's body and a man's soul. Like the child
in love with his own image and the invalid in love with
his own disease, these men of God were in love with Sin
which had come from such depths within that they believed they had created it themselves. This belief in the
immaculate conception of Sin they defended with a furious energy and stubbornly refused to assent to the possibility that culture had had any role in its creation.

They were twisted men, often fanatics, but they were
delightful companions. Many of the southern revivalists
whose names all Methodists know were guests in our
home for the duration of the August revival. These men
were remarkable storytellers, with a warm, near-riotous
sense of humor; brilliantly adept with words, soft and
gentle with the children of their host, and courteous and

considerate of their hostess. We liked them. My mother and father, neither of whom was easily drawn to the mediocre, respected them. We admired them and were influenced by them, for they had two of the essential qualities of leadership: They were free of personal anxiety, and they were close to their instinctual feelings. They were saved men. And they were sure of it. At the same time, what they were "saved from" was still accessible to them. The return of the repressed, which most of us puny folk fear as we fear the ghosts of our beloved, were to these powerful evangelists something they could whistle back at will, giants made impotent by the "power of God." No wonder they hypnotized us all!

They were fine looking men, strong, bold, with bodies of athletes. They had to be, for they put themselves through a killing routine: three sermons a day, with prayer circles before breakfast and midday dinners with the town's leading citizens at which every one gorged himself on fried chicken, corn and okra and butter beans, iced tea, peach ice cream, and lemon cheese cake; and after the evening sermon, an altar service often prolonged for hours by those under conviction of sin who agonized and prayed and yet could not secure release from their guilt. I shall never forget how I suffered with these strong men of our town—the butcher or the pitcher on the baseball team or the tenor in the choir—as they knelt there sobbing like children. Strangely enough, I cannot remember one time when the banker or millowner or principal of the school, or cotton broker or politician went to the altar. They were always among "the saved." Perhaps it is as well—for one little penitent journey might have caused a run on the bank or a cultural panic.

What an awesome gift these revivalists possessed for palpating the source of our anxiety! By means of threats, hypnotic suggestion, and a recall of the earliest fears of childhood, they plunged into our unconscious and brought up sins we had long ago forgotten. There were few of us whose souls did not pale out in the sulphurous glow of their sermons. Though they knew no word of psychoanalysis, they directed their attention to buried memories quite as much as the Freudians do, though the process was more like a butcher with a cleaver than a surgeon performing a skilled and delicate operation.

I have sometimes wondered why there were not suicides afterward, for surely enough terror and anxiety were released in unstable personalities to produce a collapse of the will to live. Perhaps we were saved from self-destruction simply because no matter how miserable and torn we were, life in Dixie seemed far better to the most unstable of us than any possible satisfactions that might accrue from succumbing to death wishes. For men believed in hell in those days and the belief restrained many a potential suicide from these acts of getting even with his world or himself. The revivals probably drove many more than we know into mental hospitals and into less conspicuous, because ambulatory, illnesses.

But when we were children, we did not analyze the motivations and consequences and costs of revivals, we accepted them. Hymns, sermons on hell, invitations (called "propositions") to come to the altar and be saved, the dirgelike singing that embroidered our nerves, the revivalist's soft whispers and prayers when one finally broke down and went scuttling to the altar—all of these phenomena we accepted with what seems, as I think of it now, a most extraordinary flexibility. There were such generous compensations: the sheet-lightning glimpses into the dark places of the human mind, the very real sense of being "saved," and scene after scene of drama and farce when an individual, strong in his refusal to give up his right to sin stood night after night adamant to the preacher's pleading though sometimes his name was called aloud.

This was strong meat for children but we loved it. There was excitement too in the setting of big tent, lanterns swinging high in the shadows, fresh clean smell of sawdust that covered the ground to make a suitable place for kneeling in prayer. There were always on the platform two pianos, and two pianos to small children were of the same exciting stuff as calliopes. There was a singer too who led the congregation with fine sweeping gestures that turned old hymns into hit tunes.

For a town whose opera house rarely had the spider webs dusted out, whose citizens depended for theater on the annual play given by the high school, and for gaiety on a minstrel show and a circus each winter, the big tent was a magnet which drew not only the rural folks but the most literate and sophisticated from Main Street.

Once in the tent, we were shown monstrosities that Mr. Barnum would not have dared exhibit to his gawking audiences. Queer misshapen vices, strange abnormal sins were marched out before our young eyes, titillating us as no circus could do. We learned about the horrors of delirium tremens and the lush pleasures those scarlet women dangle before men's eyes. *Whore, harlot, unnatural sins, self-abuse*—words we had never heard in our homes and would not have dared repeat outside the church, became an August vocabulary that was pressed deep in our memory. Adolescents, whose parents could not bring themselves to tell them where babies came from, sat on the edge of benches, wet-lipped and tense, learning rococo lessons in Sin from the revivalist who seemed magnificently experienced in such matters. The sermon titled *For Men Only* lifted the lid from the flaming pit of things one should not know. And even little girls and their mamas safe at home watched eagerly for bits of ash that might fall from the big fire.

For the adventurous, such sins as these became ir-

resistible. Any risk, even of hell, was worth running if
one could but taste of this steamy dish which the preacher
held so close, daring you, with awful threats of punishment, to touch. But for the tender-minded, the sensitive,
the dish turned to vomit, and sometimes life seemed as
nasty, as dangerous, as this portion of it with which so
many sermons were concerned. Children without one ✓
protest quietly locked doors they had almost opened,
forever shutting out life's natural spontaneous rhythms
and curiosities.

In the sermons for children which revivalists custom-
arily held in the afternoons, a lighter tone was sustained.
The presence of little girls, sitting so stiffly in front of
them with flushed-up cheeks and tight pigtails, may have
made them a bit shy about pushing matters too ruthlessly.
Or perhaps they needed to relax from their major efforts.
Whatever their reasons, they made of the children's
services rather pleasant divertisements, full of games and
animal stories. We laughed on these afternoons, I remember that. Sin was shrunken to a stature that our small
egos could cope with. The preacher quoted more from
the New Testament than from the Old, and that was a
relief. Many words about love were said, and few about
vengeance. We were told that Jesus came to earth because
God so loved the world that He gave His only begotten
Son—which seemed to us a fine thing for God to do.
We were told that Jesus loved us, that He was gentle, that
soft little lambs curled up at His feet without fear, that
He said, "Suffer little children to come unto Me." And
for one radiant, luminous moment we knew Jesus, whatever The Rest did, would never hurt us for our mistakes.
We gratefully sang, "What a Friend we have in Jesus,"
and cheerily piped, "Brighten the corner where you
are," and gradually every one of us whose viscera had
been squeezed into tight little knots by the threats of

everlasting torture heard at the grown-up services, grew limp and sleepy and went home quietly and ate a good supper.

It was late at night, after the evening sermon with its persistent propositions and compelling songs like "Almost persuaded . . . almost, but lost"; it was after the preacher had sent the town home vibrating with guilt and fear, after the grown folks were asleep and so remote from us who lay terribly awake; it was then that we remembered the threats. Then, in the darkness, hell reached out bright long red fingers and seared the edge of our beds. Sometimes we would doggedly whisper to ourselves, "We are saved too," but even as we said it, we believed ourselves liars. I remember how impossible it was for me to feel "saved." Though I went up to the altar and stayed until the revivalist pried me off my knees, I was never convinced that my kneeling had effected a change in either my present or future life. But sometimes, wanting it so badly, I lied and stood up with the rest when the evangelist asked all who were sure they would go to heaven to arise and be counted. My younger sister, more certain of her place in the family, was naturally more certain of her place in heaven, and rarely went to the altar. I remember how I admired her restraint.

But even she shivered as the Unpardonable Sin, cold, silent, implacable, slid through the room just before we fell asleep. I can feel it even now, coiling around our memories like the rattlesnakes we had seen under palmettos, daring us to believe, as we lay there listening to the rustling of our past, that we had a chance at eternal life. Whatever the theologians thought about this most cruel of ideas, which grew through the centuries into a dragon that devoured the minds of the children of Christendom, to me as a child the Unpardonable Sin had to do with one's forbidden dreams. And I think many other children shared this feeling that somehow it was tangled up with our secret hates and loves and all the passional temptations that tear at the human heart when it is three and four years old. The poets have sometimes viewed it as man's defiance of God as he stubbornly wrests from Him His knowledge of the universe, but we children thought of it more simply, and perhaps more profoundly, in terms of our own small past, and trembled, knowing our guilt.

So our learnings on sin and sex, often taught gently at home, were welded together by the flames of hell. Always we had the feeling of punishment about to fall upon us. We too were "under arrest," we too were being tried. We never knew our crime, we never saw the Authorities face to face, but we knew we would ascend from court to court to higher court, like Kafka's Joseph K., and only death would yield up the final verdict.

No wonder we feared Death as if he lived next door! For always he was slyly reaching out to snag our lives on his bony fingers if we once passed him carelessly. Graveyards full of baby dreams planted themselves in our past and stayed there, mouldering greenly. Tombstones stiffened in our minds, carving their inscriptions restlessly at night when we could not sleep. Born . . . died . . . born . . . died. We sometimes did not know how we were born, but we knew how we would die. And the littlest of us knew what might happen to us after death. Thinking of death sometimes made the living of life seem vague and shadowy as if it were no more than a few dark steps through the swamp that led toward eternal——. We could never finish that sentence. It hung in our minds, curving into a big question-mark, and sometimes wrapping itself around our spirit until we could not move.

Our old nurse would say, "Law, honey, hit'll all change

up deah. When us gets to heaven everything'll be right. Hit'll be right, honey," and she'd say it when she was moaning her own trouble with her husband or white folks and say it when she was picking sandspurs out of our bare feet. And sometimes we white children nestling close against the warm soft breasts of these strong old women could almost believe in the colored folks' heaven but more often with a passion for hopelessness we believed in the white folks' hell.

And everywhere there were the ghosts wandering restlessly through our everyday lives. Stories about haunted houses on the edge of town—what southerner does not remember!—merely took our minds off our own haunted lives and gave us reasons for our fears. We gratefully accepted the ghosts because they gave names to our fears and we urged the grown-ups to tell us again and again about them. And sometimes we learned to lay these ghosts by resurrecting them at will. We even grew fond of them as we walked the lonely curving paths across our trembling earth and felt them following us, like invisible pet dogs, wherever we went.

The physical setting for these tangled dreams and anxieties, the place we lived, was a backdrop to our Deep South childhood that seemed no more than a giant reflection of our own hearts. Back of our little town was the swamp, tangled green, oozing snakes and alligators and water lilies and sweet-blooming bays, weaving light and shadow into awful and tender designs, splotching our lives with brightness and terror. Green cypress blowing through the memory, held firmly to the past by its dark old knobby knees lost in brown water . . . rivers that go underground and creep up miles away . . . earth that shakes as you walk carefully on it, in swamp and edge of old moss-shadowed lakes.

This is the South I knew as a child. Swamp and palmetto and "sinks" and endless stretches of pines slashed and dripping their richness into little tin cups that glint like bright money. Twisting sand roads . . . warm soft sand that you play in; quicksand in which you die. Fields that flatten the eye until there is no curve left in it. Rows of crazy-leaning little grey shanties pushed over by the years. Cows wandering slow through palmetto, across the roads, mute and gaunt like the acres of stumps that do not move but stare at you like the cows. The hills were there, too, but beyond us. And beyond us were bright rolling lands that hold the sun in winter and red gullied earth so beautiful in its injury. All this is the South we remember, curving gently and more and more steeply until stopped by mountains. Beyond the mountains was the North: the Land of Damyankees, where live People Who Cause All of Our Trouble; and at the end of the North was Wall Street, that fabulous crooked canyon of evil winding endlessly through the southern mind which was like the dark race, secretly visited by those who talked loudest against it.

Our lessons were learned against this backdrop which rubbed on the senses day in, day out, confirming all that our feelings told us was true of life.

Here also, we unlearned our lessons.

3

Three Ghost Stories

THE RAVELING out of what had been woven so tightly was usually a slow process. One thread at a time came loose. Then another. Sometimes a great hole was torn by a quick stabbing experience. However it happened, it was not long in the little southerner's life before the lessons taught him as a Christian, a white man, an American, a puritan, began to contradict each other.

Sometimes, it was as if he were surrounded by characters in a bad dream who pull him this way and that, crowd him until he is almost smothered, then suddenly move in opposite directions, dragging him with them. And always, standing by, were his parents telling him this bad dream is life and he must accept it; telling him, gently or sternly, that this is reality.

But gradually, in the way of all flesh, the southern child adjusted himself to his world in which people said what they did not mean, and meant what they dared not say.

As I try to weigh the forces that pressed down on these children of my generation I know I am assuming an impossible task. Each personality creates its own gravitation system. A force that weighs heavily on one is without weight on another due to ten thousand differences in ego

114

and conscience strength, in psychic energy and that indefinable something we call the capacity for survival.

Despite these differences, most of us found it more painful to adjust to the conflict set up in our personal ✳ relationships than to warring ideas or even to the restrictions put upon bodily drives, though here again one is dealing with imponderables and perhaps it is not fruitful to compare them.

The ideas, denying each other, we could bend to with relative ease. By practicing intellectual deafness we could keep ourselves from hearing, or hearing simultaneously, the antiphonal choruses of white supremacy and democracy, brotherhood and segregation, love and lynching, and so on. The mind finds it easy to split itself into what we used to call "logic-tight compartments." This separation divorced our beliefs from the energy that might have carried them into acts, but we accepted this moral impotence as a natural thing and often developed what is called a "judicious" temperament from believing equally in both sides of a question.

The instinctual drives of the body were more difficult to cope with. These were mighty feelings and no words could have stopped them. Only a fear of consequences more violent than desire could dam up somatic urges. But our early training had given us plenty of fear—both of displeasing those we loved, and of eternal punishment. And it worked. This energy of course was only deflected —had it not found a way out, the personality would have exploded in madness. But there were outlets: [substitute satisfactions, neuroses, a thousand ways in which the personality, like a mountain stream, twisted and turned, went underground, came up again in a remote place, rushed over rocks, wasted itself, but finally reached, somehow, the end of its journey.]

This training given my generation, and its results in the shaping of personality, is different only in degree from that given most white Protestants throughout the Western world. (I separate Protestant from Catholic just here not because the training of Catholic children was less severe but because the Catholic child was given more adequate compensations for its renunciations than were given little Protestants.) But though we learned and unlearned many lessons that will seem familiar to men and women of Christian background wherever they live in the Western world, and had in common with them the same twisting love-hate-guilt ties with our parents, we of the South also have had three traumatic relationships not common outside our region, that have left a lasting impression on all of us, though few, actually, have suffered them directly.

These ghost relationships still haunt the southern mind to such an extent that many of today's most urgent problems cannot be dealt with rationally, even though the outcome of the world's crisis may depend largely upon how they are solved. They are ghosts that must be laid. Perhaps the only way to do it is to uncover them and see for ourselves the dusty nothingness beneath their masks.

These devious relationships interlock and no one of them can be understood without understanding all three. Perhaps the one that has touched most lives is the backyard temptation that pulled for a century and a half at our Anglo-American grandfathers. By the historical "accident" of slavery, our slaveholding puritan ancestors were juxtaposed to a dark people, natural, vigorous, unashamed, full of laughter and song and dance, who, without awareness that sex is "sin," had reached genital maturity. These so-called primitives (whose culture had so many sophisticated elements in it) were not, we must remember, brought into this country and hidden away in ghettos. They were brought into our back yards and left there for generations. They were everywhere, and highly conspicuous not only because of their color but because of their liveliness which the chains of slavery never subdued. From all that we know of them they seem to have had, even as some have now, a marvelous love of life and play, a physical grace and rhythm and a psychosexual vigor that must have made the white race by contrast seem washed-out and drained of much that is good and life-giving. It was natural that the white man was drawn to them. Laughter, song, rhythm, spontaneity were like a campfire in a dark tangled forest full of sins and boredom and fears. So bright, so near. . . .

But the back-yard temptation was also a menace—not so much a "menace to our women" (that poisonous idea flowered later) but a menace to the basic beliefs of white culture. In the front yard was a patriarchal system; in the back yard a matriarchy. In the front yard the lessons on sin, sex, and segregation and the overesteem of money were taught, in the back yard the children seemed always to be having recess from lessons, and for reasons no one could understand were healthy and serene in nature, less aggressive, less greedy than the white children. In the big white house a white lady was corseting her feelings and those of her children in an effort to be "pure"—and settling back finally in flabby ignorance. But in the back yard, life went on, naked and unashamed. Little black children did all the naughty things little white children were punished for, did them and prospered in body and mind. I am not forgetting that they were slaves or that they worked long hours and were brutally oppressed. I am here concerned not with how the white man treated the Negro, but with how the Negro treated himself and especially how black mothers treated their children.

I think these old black matriarchs knew secrets of child rearing and of sanity that our psychiatrists have been learning the hard way for the past sixty years through research, and that white mothers still know too little about. Unconfused by a church's rigid system of splitting spirit from body and injecting sin into bodily needs, unconfused by a patriarchal-puritanic system which psychically castrated its women, who in turn psychically castrated their children, male and female, by the burden of anxiety they laid on their minds—these women knew intuitively, or from old lore, the psychosomatic truths that we whites are groping awkwardly toward today. The results in their children were a stability, a health, a capacity for accepting strain, an exuberance, and a lack of sadism and guilt that no Anglo-Saxon group, to my knowledge, has ever shown.

It is a pity that we do not know more about it. For these were mothers who, under a harsh regime, worked the miracle of rearing children who grew up to be neither psychic slaves nor psychic rebels. Throughout the ordeal of slavery they remained people of easy dignity, kindly, humorous, bending only when necessary, deeply hurt and sad (as their spirituals make us know), but sane at the core as neither a vengeful nor a cringing people can be. They developed severe faults, of course, during these centuries. Easy lying, deceit, flattery became almost second nature to many of them. But they flattered with their tongues in their cheeks, and their "lies" turned into an art form that has contributed richly to our literature. There were the exceptions: crazed individuals who ran amok; others who turned their hate upon themselves and members of their own race with their Saturday night razor fights and quick killings over trifles; still others there were who brazenly exploited their own shame, pawning their dignity for profit. But as a group they retained an amazing stability throughout days of slavery and even through much of the long readjustment following it. That it is fast disappearing today is one of the ironic results of an "education" given in our country that does not fit psychosomatic needs of Negroes any more than it has fitted the psychosomatic needs of white people and which is rapidly transforming many Negroes, restive under severe restraints and humiliations, into as aggressive and bitter a people as are many of the white group.

But throughout slavery they possessed a psychological quality that could maturely withstand the temptation to take revenge. Their record during the Civil War and later during the chaos of Reconstruction is one of the most honorable in human annals. To call them cowards for not being vengeful, as some do today, is to ignore the dynamics of personality. Cowards would have been the first to let their hate feelings break through: it would not have required much bravery to kill and burn and rape helpless women and children left isolated on the big plantations. I think the answer lies in the home, in what happened between mother and child in those tiny slave cabins. Those of us who in our childhood knew a few of these strong old women—the children of slaves—can never forget their wisdom, their capacity for accepting life and people, their deep laughter, their unashamedness. They had strong instinctual feelings, not all of them loving, but they rarely let hate or fear master them. And I cannot imagine one of them feeling guilt in the way in which their "white folks" felt it, nor do I remember their suffering from that <u>sickness of the soul we call ambivalence</u>.

What the white race termed "savagery" in slaves who were much less cruel than their masters, was due to a method of child-rearing which was probably common to many African cultures. But to our grandfathers this "method," with its cheerful results, was a threat to their own system of punishment and sin and guilt. And yet here these black women were in the back yard, turning white beliefs into silly lies, and tempting men beyond their endurance.

Temptation and menace twisted together as they seesawed in the white man's mind. Attraction, fear, repulsion, attraction—so it went. After a few years, lighter faces began to appear in back yards. More and more light faces. And, at the same time that they were finding the back-yard temptation irresistible, these white men were declaring and sometimes beginning to believe that Negroes did not have souls, that they were not quite human, they were different, they were "no better than animals". . . . The first ghost had begun to walk through dark places in the mind of the South. *Mongrelizing* is a revealing word with connotations of broken taboos and guilt too terrible to say aloud.

These were rural people—rich and poor—many of them living far away from others of their kind, but close to the animals on farms and plantations, close to this alien race whom they refused to accept as human, yet they were breeding with them. Surely something akin to the dread felt by one who indulges in zoophilic practices must have nagged at their minds on a level rarely admitted to consciousness. What a strange ugly trap the white race made for itself! Because these slaveholders were "Christian," they felt compelled to justify the holding of slaves by denying these slaves a soul, and denying them a place in the human family. Because they were puritan, they succeeded in developing a frigidity in their white women that precluded the possibility of mutual satisfaction. Lonely and baffled and frustrated by the state of affairs they had set up in their own homes and hearts, they could not resist the vigor and kindliness and gaiety of these slaves. And succumbing to desire, they mated with these dark women whom they had dehumanized in their minds, and fathered by them children who, according to their race philosophy, were "without souls"—a strange exotic new kind of creature, whom they made slaves of and sometimes sold on the auction block. The white man's roles as slaveholder and Christian and puritan were exacting far more than the strength of his mind could sustain. Each time he found the back-yard temptation irresistible, his conscience split more deeply from his acts and his mind from things as they are.

The race-sex-sin spiral had begun. The more trails the white man made to back-yard cabins, the higher he raised his white wife on her pedestal when he returned to the big house. The higher the pedestal, the less he enjoyed her whom he had put there, for statues after all are only nice things to look at. More and more numerous became the little trails of escape from the statuary and more and more intricately they began to weave in and out of southern life. Guilt, shame, fear, lust spiralled each other. Then a time came, though it was decades later, when man's suspicion of white woman began to pull the spiral higher and higher. It was of course inevitable for him to suspect her of the sins he had committed so pleasantly and often. *What if*, he whispered, and the words were never finished. *What if.* . . . Too often white woman could only smile bleakly in reply to the unasked question. But white man mistook this empty smile for one of cryptic satisfaction and in jealous panic began to project his own sins on to the Negro male. And when he did that, a madness seized our people.

It began slowly. Fabulous stories began to be whispered of the Negro male's potency. And as white man visited more frequently the cabins in the quarters, and stayed more and more away from the big house, his suspicion grew of his wife left alone there with her embroidery and her thoughts. The more he left his sacred statuary while he sought warmer company, the more possessive became his words about her. "Our women" was a phrase that was said more and more glibly. And as suspicion and guilt grew, as minds became more paranoid, they threatened with death any white woman who dared do what they had done so freely. It is said—I am not certain that it has been proved—that a few white women did cross over the line and paid their penalty and that this penalty of death was dealt them by their own husband or father or brother as the case might be. I still find myself incredulous about this death legend. But, southern authorities like Hodding Carter and the late William Alexander Percy have, even in recent years, emphasized the strength of the taboo against white women mating with Negroes, and the heavy penalties exacted of them, at least by the community, though nowadays such women are more often banished than killed; it is the Negro male who receives the death penalty today as a "rapist" when such alliances are discovered. Perhaps only in the Mississippi delta do people still talk in such archaisms as "our women" and "men's honor," but there was a time when the South's vocabulary was heavy with such words and memories even yet are weighed down by them.

Men hungry for political and economic power could not resist exploiting this terrifying complex of guilt, anxiety, sex jealousy, and loneliness. By pumping from this vast reservoir—which had accumulated during long periods of stress—the mass hysteria they needed to irrigate their political and economic crops, they kept them green. And they are still green today, cultivated by the same system. It worked so well because the church and the home kept guilt and hate flowing into the reservoir, while the politician and business man had nothing to do but keep pumping it out. From this shocking partnership sprang other crops too, like the Ku Klux Klan and lynchings, and the massive anxieties which hardened into the rites of segregation.

If one had tried to dramatize the inward suspicion and guilt and fear that still gnaws on the white southerner's mind, it could not have been done more vividly than the Ku Klux Klan has done it for us. Pictorially, the Klan presents this Return of the Repressed in a stunning manner. White pillow case and sheet . . . the face covered . . . identity disappears and with it the conscience . . . a group stalks in silence through the "darkness" . . . a sudden abrupt appearance before the victim . . . and finally, the symbolic killing of a black male who, according to this paranoid fantasy, has "raped" a "sacred" white woman. It is a complete acting out of the white man's internal guilt and his hatred of colored man and white woman.

Historically, the first Ku Klux Klan originated in Pulaski, Tennessee, in 1866, formed by six ex-Confederate soldiers, half as a lark but used quickly afterward as an impromptu way of meeting an emergency situation in which the South was left without law-enforcing agencies. Had it actually been impromptu and accidental the idea would have been discarded and forgotten when order was restored in the South. But instead, it lived on and spread like an epidemic. Now today, more than eighty years later, the Klan rides in New Jersey as well as in Georgia and Alabama. It no longer limits itself to the revenging of "raping" and the "protecting" of womanhood nor is it turned solely against the Negro race. It is used against unions, against middle-class "deviationists," against people who "drink," against anyone who says or does anything the Klan disapproves of. It is becoming more undisguised and more undifferentiated in its sadism and intolerance, until now it is in the main a ceremonial acting-out of men's deeply repressed fantasies and deeply repressed needs for revenge and penance. It gathers under its hood the mentally ill, the haters who have forgotten what it is they hate or who dare not harm their real hate object, and also the bored and confused and ignorant. The Klan is made up of ghosts on the search for ghosts who have haunted the southern soul too long.

There are no available statistics on the frequency or range of biracial sex activities in the South. One has to rely on spotty bits of research, on case studies of southern mental patients, on whispers, and word-of-mouth revelations that go down in the South from white mother to white daughter and from colored mother to colored daughter, and on the garrulous reminiscence of white-haired colonels too old to care, and on the revealing but fragmentary research made by a few social scientists.

Regardless of statistics, this every one knows: Whenever, wherever, race relations are discussed in the United States, sex moves arm in arm with the concept of segregation. There is a union in minds, however unreal in terms of today's facts, that makes us know that the secret history of race relations in the South, the fears and the dreads, are tied up with the secret habits of southerners. We know too, that there are more than six million people of mixed Negro-white blood in our country and most of us are fairly certain that the stork did not bring them to little cotton field cabins—even though in 1940 a Georgia governor banned from state libraries a little book for children written by Dr. Karl de Schweinitz that tells where babies come from.

And now we are close to our second ghost story, which concerns the South's rejected children. When children came from these secret unions they were rarely acknowledged by their white fathers. Usually they were wholly rejected, though now and then they were secretly clung to. Most of us know stories of a white man in our community who chose not to reject his mixed children but educated them instead and helped them find a decent life for themselves. Sometimes he left these children's names in his will and posthumously made amends for human relations which in life he had not the courage to honor. This is one of the brighter threads weaving through the dark evil design of the history of the intimate life of the two races.

But these acknowledgments, though important to remember, have been few. The stark ugly fact is that millions of children have been rejected by their white fathers
and white kin and left to battle alone the giants that stalk
our culture. Little ghosts playing and laughing and weeping on the edge of the southern memory can be a haunting thing. Surely one can reject a child one has brought
into the world only by rejecting an equal part of one's
psychic life, putting a sign over it and declaring it does
not exist. White and Colored signs have had many uses
down here.

This mass rejection of children has been a heavy thing
on our region's conscience. Like a dead weight dropped
in water it lies deep in the ooze of the old and forgotten,
but when talk of change is heard, it stirs restlessly as if
still alive in its hiding place and is felt by minds innocent
of participating in the original sin but who for involved
reasons have identified themselves with it.

A few Marxists have an explanation of this widespread
miscegenation. They say it took place in the South
because the white man wanted more and more slaves and
made of slave women highly profitable economic projects
in which he invested spermatozoa. These theorists do not
even smile as they spin this odd little yarn. Indeed, to
them, there is nothing amusing about it. It is simply a
"logical" variation of the twentieth-century Story of
Creation in which, according to some, economics is the
stork that brings all things, good and bad, to this earth.
Since most of us know people to whom money and
economic power have come to mean more than love and
family and integrity and truth, it is not impossible to
believe (though our sense of humor still finds it awkward) that money lust and not body lust drove a few
planters deliberately to add to their material wealth in
this shrewd, highly pleasurable, if sadistic manner. But
the theory will impress most of us as more of an anal-

erotic daydream than a rational explanation of group behavior.

But regardless of "why," the results are well known. The men who deviated in this extralegal way were fearful lest their sons, and especially their daughters, should feel the same attraction they felt and should perhaps continue the blending of races to which they and their forefathers had made such lavish contributions. And because they feared this, knowing the strength of temptation, they blocked their children's way by erecting as many barriers as possible, extracting energy from their own guilt to build fortifications of law and custom against what they considered an "irresistible sin." Out of their confusion came that obscene word *mongrelizing* and the phrase *enforced intimate relations,* both of which were mirrors of their own shabby past. Like all criminals, they felt compelled to confess their misdeeds and did so with the naïveté of a child by the use of these words. Now today's politicians deliberately reach for these worn-out phrases when they need them to stir up excitement and fear and fantasies. Like the South's revivalists, whose place they have in large part taken in communal affairs, these politicians plunge deep into men's minds and memories, and mixing the poison of these words with the guilt already there, they produce terror—and votes.

It is all so foolish and unreal that our sense of humor and our sanity should be able to throw it off. We know conditions have changed. There are still a few casual sex relations between the races, especially in remote rural regions like the delta and in the vicinity of a few of our southern universities, but the old life in the South that bred such deep attraction is almost gone. The back-yard temptation to the front-yard puritan has disappeared, largely due to the fact that so many Negroes have become puritans themselves and back yards are farther away. The patterns of our life have changed rapidly during the

last thirty years from rural to urban because of migrations and paved roads. There are fewer personal contacts
between the races. There is now in the younger generation a freer and perhaps healthier sex life between male
and female of the white group and less necessity to seek
pleasure down the back paths. And there is a burning
blasting scorn of white men growing in the minds not
only of upper-class Negro women but of nearly every
woman of the colored race, making it a fairly dangerous
thing for a white male to approach one of them.

Yet in spite of these vast changes the old legend
persists, sustained by a stubborn memory of a now-lost
life. To understand this resurgence of fantasy I think we
have to remember that there was more to many of these
old affairs than a passing desire for exotic experience or
animal lust. Our unwritten history is full of profoundly
passionate affairs, of relationships tender and rich and
absorbing a lifetime. There were love affairs that made
white women despair as competitors; delicate, sensitive,
deep relationships in which mind and body and fantasy
met in complete union. These have existed and it would
make our southern past an impoverished thing were we
to try to erase them because of the puritanic pride of
either of the two races.

They existed because there was rich psychological soil
for them to grow in. In the old days, a white child who
had loved his colored nurse, his "mammy," with that passionate devotion which only small children feel, who had
grown used to dark velvety skin, warm deep breast, rich
soothing voice and the ease of a personality whose religion
was centered in heaven not hell, who had felt when mind
is tender the touch of a spirit almost free of sex anxiety,
found it natural to seek in adolescence and adulthood a
return of this profoundly pleasing experience. His memory was full of echoes . . . he could not rid himself of

them. And he followed these echoes to back-yard cabins, to colored town, hoping to find there the substance of shadowy memories. Sometimes he found what he sought and formed a tender, passionate, deeply satisfying relation which he was often faithful to, despite cultural barriers. But always it was a relationship without honor in his own mind and region, and the source of profound anxiety which seeped through his personality. Yet the old longing persisted, the old desire for something he could not find in his white life.

Stifled, sometimes forced into the unconscious, though betrayed ingenuously by the bathos of the "my old mammy" theme, this tender and tragic relationship of childhood—the white child and his colored nurse—has powerfully influenced the character of many southerners of the dominant class. The class is small, numerically, but out of it have come politicians, newspaper editors and journalists, college professors and presidents, doctors, preachers, industrialists, bankers, writers, governors, and their wives, and in our national government many of the prominent officials who are today determining the future of the world. It therefore seems important for us to understand this primal experience which so many leaders in world affairs and creators of American opinion have undergone in childhood.

It was customary in the South, if a family possessed a moderate income, to have a colored nurse for the children. Sometimes such a one came with the first child and lived in the family until the last one was grown. Her role in the family was involved and of tangled contradictions. She always knew her "place," but neither she nor her employers could have defined it. She was given a limited authority, but it was elastic enough to stretch into dictatorship over not only children but the white mother and sometimes even the male head of the family. They leaned on her strength because they had so little of their own or because she had so much, and once leaning they could not free themselves from subjection. Many an old nurse, knowing all there was to know of her white folks, familiar with every bone of every skeleton in their closets, gradually became so dominating that her employers actually feared her power. Yet she was a necessary part of these big sprawling households; her knowledge, alone, of how to grow children was too precious a thing to throw away lightly, and her value extended far beyond child rearing. She nursed old and young when they were sick, counseled them when they were unhappy, took the problem child at least out of earshot, and in crises her biologically rooted humor had a magic way of sweeping white clouds away. She was nurse, witch doctor, and priest, conjuring off our warts, our stomach-aches and fears, all of which disappeared when she said they would. She knew wonderful simples for ailments of body and soul, and bound up both in earthy ointments. We put on undershirts, come fall, as she told us to, hung asafetida bags around our necks when there were epidemics in town, ate sulphur and cream of tartar each spring, stayed away from graveyards after dark as she taught us to do, wouldn't have dared iron anything on Sunday, and following her precepts we prospered as did her own children. Sometimes Mr. White Man himself did not deem it beneath him to call on her for help. "Mammy, come in here and talk to Miss Sarah [his wife]. Talk sense to her, Mammy," and he'd leave for the cotton gin downtown or the sawmill, hoping to God that Mammy could straighten Sarah out. And usually she did, and Sarah would be as meek and gentle as a wife should be when her husband returned that evening.

In many homes, the nurse was also a wet nurse. We were children in the pre-refrigerator age and bottle feeding was a perilous business. It was much safer when mother's milk disagreed, to turn an ailing or malnourished infant over to a nurse whose ample breasts could take care of another as well as her own. It was not a rare sight in my generation to see a black woman with a dark baby at one breast and a white one at the other, rocking them both in her wide lap, shushing them to sleep as she hummed her old songs. Still swinging them from side to side in her arms, she would lay them down on the same pallet underneath a shade tree and leave them there, little black little white together, sleeping in peace. These intimacies fill our memories and do strange things now to our segregated grown-up lives.

In my home, our nurse lived in the back yard beyond Mother's flower garden in a small cabin whose interior walls were papered with newspapers. Much of my very young life was spent there. I was turned over to her when a new baby took my place in the family. And because I seemed not to have the stamina to adjust to this little intruder I protested by refusing to eat and kept up a food strike so long that they grew alarmed and called in the doctor although Aunt Chloe looked on, they say, with obvious scorn at their panic. And after the doctor left his prescription and drove away in his buggy, she took me to her cabin and kept me there. The story is that Aunt Chloe tried food after food all of which I rejected, then studying the pale young face before her for a little, she took a little food, chewed it first in her mouth, put it in mine and I swallowed it promptly. Soon I was prospering on this fine psychological diet, gaining in weight and security as the weeks went by. I was once more the center of somebody's universe. What did it matter that this universe encompassed only one room in a little back-yard cabin? It filled my need and I loved her.

Such a relationship with such a woman is not to be brushed off by the semantic trick of labelling her a "nurse."

Sometimes these nurses took over the care of a baby on

the day it was born. More often Mammy entered a child's life in an important way at the painful moment when a new baby had taken its place. Wounded and hurt, feeling as profound a rejection as the human heart knows, we were taken into her life, where she made us feel welcome and prized. In her own way and not wholly according to what the psychiatrists of today would suggest, she helped us adjust to the one who had taken our place, nursed us through and sometimes, not always, weaned us from this experience that grasped like nettles and threatened to hold us to it for the rest of our lives. But though freed from this, we were tied fast to another, even more difficult, relationship.

Psychoanalysts have made us know during the past fifty years how the deep injuries to the infant psyche can leave scar tissue that binds a personality for a lifetime. We have grown used to words we do not always understand: the Oedipus complex, "fixation," and the pictures of rejection that haunt the child memory. But this dual relationship which so many white southerners have had with two mothers, one white and one colored and each of a different culture that centered in different human values, makes the Oedipus complex seem by comparison almost a simple adjustment.

Before the ego had gained strength, just as he is reaching out to make his first ties with the human family, this small white child learns to love both mother and nurse; he is never certain which he loves better. Sometimes, secretly, it is his "colored mother" who meets his infantile needs more completely, for his "white mother" is busy with her social life or her older children or perhaps a new one, and cannot give him the time and concern he hungers for. Yet before he knows words, he dimly perceives that his white mother has priority over his colored mother, that somehow he "belongs" more to her, though he may stay more with the other. But he is satisfied with things

as they are, for his colored mother meets his immediate
needs as he hungers to have them met. She is easy, per-
missive, less afraid of simple earthy biological needs and
manifestations. When naughtiness must be punished, it is
not hers but the white mother's prerogative to do so; and
afterward, little white child runs back to colored mother
for comfort and sugar-tits. Sometimes, white child hates
white mother after this ordeal, and clings desperately to
his colored mother, who soothes him and gives him a tea
cake as she softly asks him, "Ain' you shamed, honey, to
be so bad!" And he is shamed, and confused, and sometimes very lonely also.

And now curious things happen. Strong bonds begin to
grow as the most profound relationships of his life are
formed, holding him to two women whose paths will take
them far from each other. It is as if he were fastened to
two umbilical cords which wrap themselves together in
a terrifying tangle, and then suddenly, inexplicably, but
with awful sureness, begin steadily to move, each in a different direction. Because white mother has always set up
right and wrong, has with authority established the "do"
and the "don't" of behavior, his conscience, as it grows
in him, ties its allegiance to her and to the white culture
and authority which she and his father represent. But to
colored mother, persuasive in her relaxed attitude toward
"sin," easy and warm in her physical ministrations, generous with her petting, he ties his pleasure feelings.

Big white house, little cabin, enter the picture he is
slowly forming in his mind about this strange world he
lives in, and both begin subtly to give pattern to it. A
separation has begun, a crack that extends deep into his
personality. He erects "white" image-ideals and secretly
pulls them down again. He says aloud what his heart
denies stubbornly. Part of him stays more and more in
the world he "belongs" in; part of him stays forever in
the world he dare not acknowledge. He feels deep tender-

ness for his colored nurse and pleasure in being with her, but he begins to admire more and more the lovely lady who is his "real" mother. He is impressed by her white beauty, her clothes and grace and charm; he feels one with the big powerful man who is his father—though he fears him too and sometimes secretly hates him—and one with the tradition that stands like the big house he was born in, always there before him as "his." But when he is miserable, he creeps away and crawls up in old black arms, every curve of which he has known by heart since babyhood, and snuggles against a cotton dress that is ragged maybe but will always smell good to his memory. . . . Sometimes he wants to stay in her lap forever; but he slips away shamefaced, remembering *this* mother is not "fitten," as she says herself, to sit in the living room and eat at the table with the rest of the family. He is learning a desolating lesson that shrinks the heart when we think of its human implications; and soon he will know it too well ever to forget it.

His "white" conscience, now, is hacking at his early love life, splitting it off more and more sharply into acceptable and unacceptable, what is done and what isn't; into "pure" and "impure"; Madonna and whore; Mother and nurse; wife and prostitute; white conscience and colored pleasures; marriage and lust; "right" and "wrong"; belief and act; segregation and brotherhood. He accords his mother the esteem and respect that are hers; he feels more and more a pulling obligation to her, though he does not know why. And after a time, he feels that he "owes" her so much that he steals the adoration which he had conferred upon his colored mother long ago, and returns it to his white mother as rightfully hers. From now on, his gifts to his old nurse will be little presents, not of esteem and love, but a linen handkerchief or a check at Christmas and birthday, and all his life long, tears when old spirituals are sung. . . .

He has almost completed the cheapening of this tender profound relationship which his culture insists upon. The segregation of his first love feelings is nearly perfected, but not quite; not ever is it quite finished. Deep down in him, he often reserves his play, his "real" pleasure, his relaxed enjoyment of sex activities, and his fantasy, for women as much like his nurse (they may or may not have colored skin) as his later life can discover. Now he has achieved his stature as a white man; he has accepted the life that his whiteness conferred upon him. But he is never at ease. The powerful drives of childhood will not stay in the little stream beds his culture gullied out for them. Again and again they overflow, sweeping across him like a flood. Tenderness for his mother turns into sudden cruelty for his wife which he conceals even from himself sometimes, or betrays by lightning flashes of hatred. Sometimes he loses the shame he is trained to feel about women of other color or class and admits to himself and to others his pleasure in them. Sometimes a sweeping sadistic feeling for all women overpowers him. He feels betrayed, cheated; and he despises himself and them for a treacherous partnership in which he seems always to have been the loser since childhood. And in deep repugnance, he sometimes turns away from all women, shunning them white and black, and spends his real feelings on men and his hours in companionship with them, or centers his energy on making money, more and more money.

However they dealt with it, nearly all men—and women —of the dominant class in the South suffered not only the usual painful experiences of growing up in America but this special southern trauma in which segregation not only divided the races but divided the white child's heart.

Three ghost relationships—white man and colored woman, white father and colored children, white child and his beloved colored nurse—haunting the mind of the

South and giving shape to our lives and our souls.

And there was a fourth, poisoned by disesteem as were the others, yet a relationship that held the good qualities of one person firmly to the good of another. Back-yard though it was, lopsided by color, curiously belittled by those who valued it most, this friendship between individuals of the two races was a thing of grace and mutual concern. Begun in childhood, it sometimes was broken only by death. Shamefaced though they were in its presence, men white and colored often sacrificed themselves in its name. This friendship across barriers has been, of all bi-racial relationships in the South, the one most enriching in its human qualities; and one that has restrained the region from insane excesses of prejudice. It nourished no guilt, sheltered no hate, was not used as an escape from responsibilities. It was no ghost, but a real thing that bound men one to another though there was between them a deep chasm that drained away much that is good from the lives of both. There was no honor in that relationship but there was a secret acceptance of each other as human. And it became a green growing thing in that desert which disesteem and lack of responsibility had made of the southerner's human relations.

I remember, as a child, the bitterness on faces of my father's and grandfather's friends and other men on Main Street in the little town where I was reared. Quick, hearty laughter and so few warm smiles. . . . I remember the easy tears in hard old eyes and unhappy lips and weathered faces, reddened by sun in the sensitive way of Scotch-Irish skins. I remember mouths moving restlessly, chewing tobacco, smoking a pipe, munching a straw, or cursing, or saying low words to other men as eyes lingered on hard young female buttocks sashaying down bright streets. There would be laughter, mirthless, oozing uncleanliness. And then the old men would turn, and seeing little school children watching them gravely, they would in the way of grown-ups give them a stick of candy from the store counter or hand them a nickel and tell them to buy themselves a cold drink or a package of chewing gum. . . .

Those faces on Main Street shaded by wide straw hats are surrounded in my child-memory by hardware and ploughs, seed bags and bales of cotton, the smell of guano and mule lots, hot sun on sidewalks and lovely white ladies with sweet childlike voices and smooth childlike faces, and old gardens of boxwood and camellias, and fields endlessly curving around my small world. I know now that the bitterness, the cruel sensual lips, the quick tears in hard eyes, the sashaying buttocks of brown girls, the thin childish voices of white women, had a great deal to do with high interest at the bank and low wages in the mills and gullied fields and lynchings and Ku Klux Klan and segregation and sacred womanhood and revivals, and Prohibition. And that no part of this memory can be understood without recalling all of it.

There were other faces, and I remember them also—in church, office, library, or school, or newspaper office. Tired faces, often, and of a slow charm, and gentle, with voice soft-spoken and of profound hesitation, or sometimes urbane and witty. These were the faces you saw of men who feared the "outbreak of violence," who wrote editorials suggesting things must change slowly, who read poetry or wrote it, who said, "You can't turn the South upside down overnight," who said, "Whatever is done for the Negro—and things should be done—must be done under the system of segregation we have lived under all of our lives." These faces belonged to men loyal to their "white mothers" and loyal in a secret, deep-rooted way, to their dark ones also; loyal above all else to the conscience their mothers gave them, men who clung to their white culture as a cripple clings to his crutches; whose passion and memories had been deeply repressed, and who had put up signs long ago in their unconscious and had forbidden themselves ever to trespass them.

Tired liberals. Remembering them now and my own generation's good will and blindness, I find myself wondering if Mammy in Dixie and Nanny in England have ever been given their due credit for the rise of Anglo-Saxon liberalism—not only in its tortured form but in its best manifestations of moderation and justice and mercy and value of human life.

There were those also, who could neither successfully repress their feelings nor give outlet to them; whose minds and hearts, whose hate and love were in never-ceasing combat that drained all strength away: our small-town failures from the best families . . . and some of the most lovable and charming men on earth.

And there were the few who were different, who somehow found a center around which to build their lives and their region. These gave us our strength, held us back from too much self-pity, reached out for the new, made great errors and achieved real triumphs. There were not many, but our region cannot forget them for they were those who carried out their beliefs, limited as these beliefs were, and refused to bow down to confusion.

But even these men did not see what segregation had done to the South's women, pushed away on that lonely pedestal called Sacred Womanhood.

4

The Women

OF ALL the humiliating experiences which southern white women have endured, the least easy to accept, I think, was that of a mother who had no choice but to take the husk of a love which her son in his earliest years had given to another woman. She valiantly made jokes about it, telling her friends that her child preferred Mammy to her and that was fine, wasn't it, for it gave her so much more time to attend to all she had to do! "I don't know how I could have done without her," she would say and laugh a light tinkling laugh which sounded like little glass bells about to break into splinters. "Mammy was wonderful," she'd say. "I just don't see how we could do without the colored folks, do you?" she'd say. "I declare! but aren't the younger ones trifling —now look at that Emmy, doing nothing but rolling a dip stick around in her mouth and humming and with her shoes off again! But when I hear men say, 'Send 'em all back to Africa,' I say they don't have the housework to do, why we couldn't possibly . . . Oh, my!" sighing and laughing, and trying to forget things she could never forget.

This giving up of one's men and one's childhood to colored women—for the girl-child was shaped as subtly as little boys by the nurse-mother relationship—took on the unreal, shadowy quality of a dream; a recurring dream that southern white women could not rid themselves of. One's self . . . one's father . . . one's husband . . . one's son. . . . Sometimes in the old days it made a pattern like that: a stark dance which all their life they tread the bleak measures of, with heart and body too rigid to make of space anything but a thin line to hold to.

A secret wound that can never be shown is not tragedy for tragedy finds its stature on a stage where it can feel beyond it, its audience. To these women their life was only a shameful sore that could not be acknowledged.

Sometimes they could weep. A soundless weeping that trickled down into the crevices of personality leaving damp little places for thorns to grow, and sometimes for pale ghostly flowers that gave a fragrance of death to certain women. You remember these women from your childhood, and as you remember you keep thinking of lost graveyards under oak trees where moss swings in the still air as if to the heartbeat of the dead, and small carved lambs watch over baby mounds; you keep thinking of cape jasmine in your mother's back yard, and the way you felt in the night when you awoke after dreams and smelled the night-blooming cereus below the window. . . .

It was as if these women never quite left the presence of the dead but mourned gently and continuously a loss they could not bear to know the extent of. Unable to look at the ugly facts of their life, they learned to see mysterious things the rest of us could not see. I remember how they "felt" premonitions, counting shadows and making of them cryptic answers. They "dreamed" that a beloved one would die and the beloved sometimes died. They "felt" there would be no returning when one left on a long journey and sometimes there was no return. They chanted so sweetly the death-knell of those they loved that I remember how carefully I avoided these friends of my mother's who dwelt serenely among disasters, for I feared that one day a gentle Cassandra might hold the syllables of my name on her tongue.

The little ghost women of small southern towns . . . swishing into church, sometimes singing in the choir, slipping like their own carefully made custards down the dark maw of life. Their number was few. One remembers them because they roam even now restlessly through time.

I think, however, that most women of my mother's age, though their characters were twisted and shaped by these troubles, retained a more earthy quality and a firm grasp indeed on things of this world. The pain they denied or tried to displace. This emptiness was the natural way women should feel! Like childbirth pangs and menstrual cramps, the sexual blankness of their life was "God's way" and hence if you were sensible must be accepted. But some stubbornly called it "female trouble" and went to doctors' offices as often as to church, to moan their misery.

A few "solved it all" by rejecting their womanly qualities. They seemed to envy men their freedom from pain and their access to pleasure. And sometimes they hated their own Maker too (a blasphemy they carefully hid) for giving females the long agony of parturition and none of the male's quick ecstasy of procreation. Yet there was usually a curious loyalty to their own father, though every other man was not "fit to be lived with." In later decades, when women were freer, these protesters turned toward the cities, gathering together, a grim little number, cropping their hair short, walking in heavy awkward strides, and acquiring, as do subjugated people who protest their chains, the more unpleasant qualities of their enemy. Not daring in the secret places of their minds to confess what they really wanted, they demanded to be treated "exactly like men." They were of course a part of the

psychosexual, economic, political protest of women aris-
ing throughout Western culture, a kind of fibroid growth
of sick cells multiplying aggressiveness in an attempt at
cure. But there was no comfortable place for such women
in the South, though a few lived in every town.

The majority of southern women convinced themselves
that God had ordained that they be deprived of pleasure,
and meekly stuffed their hollowness with piety, trying to
believe the tightness they felt was hunger satisfied. Cul-
turally stunted by a region that still pays nice rewards to
simple-mindedness in females, they had no defense against
blandishment. They listened to the round words of men's
tribute to Sacred Womanhood and believed, thinking no
doubt that if they were not sacred then what under God's
heaven *was* the matter with them! Once hoisted up by the
old colonels' oratory, they stayed on lonely pedestals and
rigidly played "statue" while their men went about more
important affairs elsewhere.

These women turned away from the ugliness which
they felt powerless to cope with and made for themselves
and their families what they called a "normal" life. Their
homes, often simple, were gracious and good to live in.
The South—if one can forget the shabby milltowns, the
rickety Colored Towns, the surrealist city tenements—
is full of such homes. Places you remember—if you live
on that side of town—of quiet ease and comfort and taste.
In these homes, food and flowers were cherished, and old
furniture, and the family's past (screened of all but the
pleasing and the trivial). Sex was pushed out through the
back door as a shameful thing never to be mentioned.
Segregation was pushed out of sight also, and this was
managed so successfully that until the last few decades
most white southerners cheerfully said there was no race
problem for it had been "solved." Out through the back
door went the unpleasant and unmentionable; in through
the back door came trays laden with food as delicious as

can be found in the world. Though puritanism controlled the regions left out of the physiology books, and Prohibition succeeded sometimes in banishing the bottle, the groaning table was left free.

Whatever the hurt in our lives, there are these memories of food, and flowers, and of southern gardens, filled with our mothers' fantasies that had no other way to creep into life. We are always remembering a face and the longing in it as plants were set in damp ground and shaded against the sun. . . . A figure stooping, familiar hands feeling around in warm soft dirt to slip a weed out, planting and transplanting little secret dreams, making them live in an azalea, a rose, a camellia, when they could not live in her own arid time. . . . A voice grown plaintive over a peaked little plant that refused to bloom . . . so softly scolding the flowers for not living life to its full. In the mornings these old gardens full of lively bugs, and toads hopping among the violets, and new blow-y spider webs that never break in the memory, were like a clear mind filled with bright dewy ideas. But at night in the moonlight, a woman walking alone, up and down prim rows of camellias or in summer among the lilies, even now can make one want to close the gates against the past forever—so hurting is the realization of an emptiness that need not have been.

With their gardens and their homes, these women tried to shut out evil, and sometimes succeeded only in sheltering their children from good. If you could just keep from them the things that must never be mentioned, all would be well! Innocence, virtue, ignorance, silence were synonyms twining around young lives like smilax. It was not evil but the knowledge of it that injured, these mothers believed. What you don't hear or read or see surely can never be known to you. And because they did not believe things *could* change or that they should (though they could not have told you why) they had to shut their minds against knowledge of what existed. They could not let their imaginations feel the sorrow of a colored mother whose child is shamed from birth, nor once look deep into poverty, nor once touch the agony of a back-door life lived forever and ever, nor once realize what they themselves had been deprived of. They could not have borne it. And because they could not let themselves know, they were terrified at a word, a suggestion, anything that caused them to feel deeply. It was as if one question asked aloud might, like a bulldozer, uproot their garden of fantasies and tear it out of time, leaving only naked bleeding reality to live with.

There were others whose minds perhaps were not brighter, but whose natures could not accept life so meekly. They felt compelled to question and to answer their own questions. They would not have used the word "sex" aloud, but their questions and answers told them that all a woman can expect from lingering on exalted heights is a hard chill afterward; that indeed, white women had not profited in the least from the psychosexual profit system which segregation in the South supported so lavishly; and that furthermore, no bargain had been made with them in any of these transactions. They learned that *discrimination* was a word with secret meanings and they did not like its secrets. This much of semantics they understood as clearly as their recipe for beaten biscuits. In the white southern woman's dictionary, *discrimination* could be defined as a painful way of life which too often left an empty place in her bed and an ache in the heart. Whether or not these women had themselves experienced this pain—and we must remember that many had not— they knew segregation in the South had cleaved through white woman's tenderest dreams. They had seen it turn a life drama of child, wife, mother into tragedy, or more often into plain vulgar melodrama. How could they sit in the audience and applaud their own humiliation?

So, they climbed down from the pedestal when no one was looking and explored a bit. Not as you may think, perhaps. They were conventional, highly "moral" women, who would not have dreamed of breaking the letter of their marriage vows or, when not married, their technical chastity. But their minds went a-roaming and their sympathies attached themselves like hungry little fibers to all kinds of people and causes while their shrewd common sense kicked old lies around until they were popping like firecrackers.

These ladies went forth to commit treason against a southern tradition set up by men who had betrayed their mothers, sometimes themselves, and many of the South's children white and mixed, for three long centuries. It was truly a subversive affair, but as decorously conducted as an afternoon walk taken by the students of a Female Institute. It started stealthily, in my mother's day. Shyly, these first women sneaked down from their chilly places, did their little sabotage and sneaked up again, wrapping innocence around them like a lace shawl. They set secret time bombs and went back to their needlework, serenely awaiting the blast. They had no lady Lincoln to proclaim their emancipation from southern tradition but they scarcely needed one.

The thing was a spontaneous reaction. Mother in her old age told daughter strange truths that had gnawed on her lonely heart too long. And daughter told other women. Colored and white women stirring up a lemon-cheese cake for the hungry males in the household looked deep into each other's eyes and understood their common past. A mistress, reading the Bible to her colored maid polishing silver, would lay aside Holy Writ and talk of things less holy but of immense importance to both of them.

Insurrection was on. White men were unaware of it,

but the old pedestal on which their women had been safely stowed away, was reeling and rocking. With an emotionally induced stupidity really beneath them, these men went on with their race-economic exploitation, protecting themselves behind rusty shields of as phony a moral cause as the Anglo-American world has ever witnessed. In the name of *sacred womanhood*, of *purity*, of *preserving the home*, lecherous old men and young ones, reeking with impurities, who had violated the home since they were sixteen years old, whipped up lynchings, organized Klans, burned crosses, aroused the poor and ignorant to wild excitement by an obscene, perverse imagery describing the "menace" of Negro men hiding behind every cypress waiting to rape "our" women. In the name of such holiness, they did these things to keep the affairs of their own heart and conscience and home, as well as the community, "under control." And not once did they dream their women did not believe their lies.

And then it happened. The lady insurrectionists gathered together in one of our southern cities. They primly called themselves church women but churches were forgotten by everybody when they spoke their revolutionary words. They said calmly that they were not afraid of being raped; as for their sacredness, they could take care of it themselves; they did not need the chivalry of a lynching to protect them and did not want it. Not only that, they continued, but they would personally do everything in their power to keep any Negro from being lynched and furthermore, they squeaked bravely, they had plenty of power.

They had more than they knew. They had the power of spiritual blackmail over a large part of the white South. All they had to do was drop their little bucket into any one of numerous wells of guilt dotting the landscape and splash it around a bit. No one, of thousands of white men, had any notion how much or how little each woman knew about his private goings-on. Some who had never been guilty in act began to equate adolescent fantasies with reality, and there was confusion everywhere.

This was in 1930. These women organized an Association of Southern Women for the Prevention of Lynching. Their husbands, sons, brothers, and uncles often worked by their side; many of them with sincere concern for the state of affairs, others because they had to.

It may seem incredible, but the custom of lynching had rarely been questioned by the white group. The church women's action gave a genuine shock. This was a new thing in Dixie. The ladies' valor is not diminished, I think, by reminding ourselves that the movement could not have crystallized so early had not Dr. Will Alexander, and a handful of men and women whom he gathered around him, pushed things off to a good start in 1918 with the first interracial committee in the South. There were other yeasty forces at work: A world war had squeezed and pulled the earth's people apart and squeezed them together again; the Negroes themselves, led by courageous men like Walter White of Atlanta and W. E. B. Du Bois and their northern white friends were making our nation aware that Negroes have rights; the group around Dr. Howard Odum—whose first study of the Negro in 1910 greatly influenced social science's interest in Negro-white patterns of life—were gathering all kinds of facts concerning a region that had been for so long content with its fantasies and fears. The women's role was to bake the first pan of bread made from this rising batter, and to serve it hot as is southern custom.

After this magnificent uprising against the sleazy thing called "chivalry," these women worked like the neat, industrious housewives they really were, using their mops and brooms to clean up a dirty spot here and there but with no real attempt to change this way of life which they dimly realized had injured themselves and their children

as much as it had injured Negroes, but which they nevertheless clung to.

Of course the demagogues would have loved to call
them "Communists" or "bolsheviks," but how could they?
The women were too prim and neat and sweet and lady-
like and churchly in their activities, and too many of them
were the wives of the most powerful men in town. Indeed, the ladies themselves hated the word "radical" and
were quick to turn against anyone who dared go further
than they in this housecleaning of Dixie. Few of them
had disciplined intellects or giant imaginations and probably no one of them grasped the full implications of this
sex-race-religion-economics tangle, but they had warm
hearts and powerful energy and a nice technic for bargaining, and many an old cagey politician, and a young
one or two, have been outwitted by their soft bending
words.

They followed a sound feminine intuition, working as
"church women," leaning on the strength of Christ's
teachings for support when they needed it. They worked
with great bravery but so unobtrusively that even today
many southerners know little about them. But they
aroused the conscience of the South and the whole country about lynching; they tore a big piece of this evil out
of southern tradition, leaving a hole which no sane man
in Dixie now dares stuff up with public defenses. They
attacked the KKK when few except the editors of the
Columbus (Georgia) *Enquirer*, among white southern
newspaper men, had criticized this group from whom
Hitler surely learned so much.

But they were not yet done. They had a few more
spots to rub out. One had to do with their own souls.
They believed that the Lord's Supper is a holy sacrament
which Christians cannot take without sacrilege unless
they will also break bread with fellow men of other color.
Believing, they put on their best bib and tucker and

gathered in small groups to eat with colored women, deliberately breaking a taboo that had collected many deep fears around it.

It is difficult for those not reared as white southerners to remember how this eating taboo in childhood was woven into the mesh of things that are "wrong," how it pulled anxieties from stronger prohibitions and attached them to itself. But we who live here cannot forget. One of these church women told me of her first eating experience with colored friends. Though her conscience was serene, and her enjoyment of this association was real, yet she was seized by an acute nausea which disappeared only when the meal was finished. She was too honest to attribute it to anything other than anxiety welling up from the "bottom of her personality," as she expressed it, creeping back from her childhood training. Others have told me similar experiences: of feeling "pangs of conscience," as one put it, "though my conscience was clearly approving"; or suddenly in the night awaking, overwhelmed by "serious doubts of the wisdom of what we are doing."

The white women were not alone in these irrational reactions. Colored women also found it hard, but for different reasons. Sometimes their pride was deeply hurt that white women felt so virtuous when eating with them. They were too sensitive not to be aware of the psychic price the white women paid for this forbidden act, and yet too ignorant of the training given white children to understand why there had to be a price. And sometimes the colored women were themselves almost overcome by a break-through not of guilt but of their old repressed hatred of white people. One of the most charming, sensitive, intelligent Negro women I know, tells me that even now when she is long with white people she grows physically ill and has immense difficulty coming to terms with the resentments of her childhood.

To break bread together, each group had to force its way through thick psychological barriers, and each did it with little understanding of their own or the other group's feelings. When anxieties appeared, most of the church women, white and Negro, suppressed them firmly by laying the ponderous weight of the New Testament on them, declaring bravely that "Jesus would have done likewise."

In more recent years this group, united with the church women in all parts of the nation and from most of our denominations, has taken a stand against segregation in the church. The same group in Atlanta whose nucleus was for years under Dorothy Tilly's fine leadership has made a brave stand against segregation in colleges, schools, churches and interstate travel. They are daring more these days, doing fewer paint jobs and more carpentry on the old Southern Mansion, adding rooms for the rest of the family. And because they are, they are not receiving the indulgence of newspapers and politicians they once had. Perhaps their blackmailing power has waned. Perhaps they are developing new powers and are beginning to be feared in new ways. However much or little they have accomplished (and sometimes it seems small set against the size and urgency of the job), these church women at least have spread a green-growing cover crop on the South's worn-out spiritual soil. In that lovely and rare way of human nature, they pushed aside their own trouble and somehow grew strong enough to reach out with compassion toward those more miserable. It seemed almost as if they lifted their natures by their own leverage though they would say that it was their faith in the teachings of Jesus that lifted them.

It would be pleasant to stop the story of the women here, but there is a more tragic page.

Like their men, many of them found it easier to cultivate hate than love. Their own dreams destroyed, they destroyed in cruelty their children's dreams and their men's aspirations.

It was a compulsive thing. Rarely were they aware of the hate compelling them to do it. Most of them felt they were doing "right." Most of them thought it was their duty to watch over the morals of their children and husbands. They did not see themselves in the ungracious role of exacting of their family the same obedience to the same Authority which had exacted so much of them.

The little thorns growing deep in secret wounds thrust up sharp points into their conscience, making it a prickly thing, but they covered it with the soft folds of affectionate concern and hid from themselves the thorn tips. When they turned this conscience against their children, or the men in their family, they thought they were doing God's will. And, as is the way of humans, in the name of "what is right" they committed as great evil at home as did their men in the name of Sacred Womanhood over in Colored Town or at the state capitals.

Many a man went into politics, or joined the KKK, had a nervous breakdown or forged checks, got drunk or built up a great industry, because he could no longer bear the police-state set up in his own home. But this would have been a hard thing for these good mothers and wives to believe, and for the men also.

As time passed, mothers went more and more compulsively about the training of their children: imposing rigidities on spirit and mind, imposing eating schedules as if eating were a duty, elimination schedules as if elimination were a responsibility one owed to one's state, hurrying weaning as if suckling were an immoral habit which babies must give up as soon as possible, binding the curiosity of childhood as the Chinese once bound their little girls' feet.

More and more rigid became this training and more

impersonal. It was all such a desperate business. If they had been asked what they feared they would have been unable to answer. They sometimes had tears but no words for their anxiety. They only knew they must keep their children pure and innocent, they must "make" them good. There was inside each little body, inside each mind, a powerful force: if let out, it might blast their children's "morals" to pieces. They were compelled, therefore, to wall up this danger. So they armored their children against their fantasies and feelings, preparing them for human relations as if for a cruel medieval battle.

This training, until recent decades, was often complicated by the child's dual Mother-Mammy relationship. For sometimes Mother would give orders which Mammy, more wise in the ways of childhood, would not carry out. Many a child of my generation was split in his moral nature, as in his first human relationships, by a white mother's code which colored nurse intuitively knew was too rigid and unreal for the warm, pliant human spirit to adhere to.

We cannot forget that their culture had stripped these white mothers of profound biological rights, had ripped off their inherent dignity and made them silly statues and psychic children, stunting their capacity for understanding and enjoyment of husbands and family. It is not strange that they became vigilant guardians of a southern tradition which in guarding they often, unbeknownst to their own minds, avenged themselves on with a Medea-like hatred.

In many there was a profound subservience; they dared not question what had injured them so much. It was all wrapped up in one package: sex taboos, race segregation, "the right to make money the way Father made money," the duty to go to church, the fear of new knowledge that would shake old beliefs, the splitting of ideals from actions —and you accepted it all uncritically. You insisted on others accepting it also. You dreaded a deviationist, you were in terror lest your children be other than orthodox southerners. You used your conscience as if it were a hypodermic needle, plunging it into the tenderest spots of young spirits, filling them with your guilt, hoping to inoculate them "for their own good" against vague, dread "evils."

But it was a tainted needle.

It would be as unfair to blame the mothers of two or three generations for a way of life that began destroying its children long before they were born, as it would be to blame the men. Both men and women were born into it and of it. And because it was a culture that lacked almost completely the self-changing power that comes from honest criticism, because in the past it forced out its children who saw dangers and tried to avert them, who had insight and talents that could have contributed so richly to the South's recovery; because it bruised those who grimly stayed, unwelcomed, until their energies were depleted (we have only to recall the many poets, teachers, novelists, who were forced to leave or else were smothered and forgotten)—because it did these things to its own men, it is not difficult to understand why these women, our mothers and perhaps ourselves, could not do other than bend to the system and think it "right" to bend to it. They did not have enough insight—where could they have got it?—to grow wary of a conscience that drives ruthlessly across natural, spontaneous needs. They did not dream the energy driving this conscience might be hate, not love. They could not have accepted the fact that their own banned desires had slipped into their conscience giving it its cruel power. They had not questioned life closely enough—for life gave harsh answers—to discover that guilt and ideals are as different sometimes as the insane and the sane.

We cannot censure—who would dare!—but we know now that these women, forced by their culture and their heartbreak, did a thorough job of closing the path to mature genitality for many of their sons and daughters, and an equally good job of leaving little cleared detours that led downhill to homosexual and infantile green pastures, and on to alcoholism, neuroses, divorce, to race-hate and brutality, and to a tight inflexible mind that could not question itself.

They did a thorough job of dishonoring curiosity, of making honesty seem a treasonable thing, of leaving in their children an unquenchable need to feel superior to others, to bow easily to authority, and to value power and money more dearly than human relations and love.

They did a thorough job of splitting the soul in two. They separated ideals from acts, beliefs from knowledge, and turned their children sometimes into exploiters but more often into moral weaklings who daydream about democracy and human dignity and freedom and integrity, yet cannot find the real desire to bring these dreams into reality; always they keep dreaming and hoping, and fearing, that the next generation will do it.

Sometimes we blame Mom too much for all that is wrong with her sons and daughters. After all, we might well ask, who started the grim mess? Who long ago made Mom and her sex "inferior" and stripped her of her economic and political and sexual rights? Who, nearly two thousand years ago, said, "It is good for a man not to touch a woman. . . . But if they cannot contain, let them marry: for it is better to marry than to burn"? Certainly that old misogynist St. Paul was no female apostle. Man, born of woman, has found it a hard thing to forgive her for giving him birth. The patriarchal protest against the ancient matriarch has borne strange fruit through the years. . . .

In speaking of millions of people and their customs, their feelings and values it is well to remember that many have not shared in experiences that have affected their whole lives. They have, instead, made identification with them. Experiences which others have had link themselves sometimes with our secret fantasies and needs until a curious bond is woven of the actual experiences of the few and the unconscious desire of the many to possess them. A generation free of wounds will identify itself with the battle scars of a past generation in a masochistic community of daydreams because it needs to feel pain. Hanns Sachs has reminded us in *The Creative Unconscious* of man's capacity to daydream in collaboration with others when each has within him the same secret fantasy. Here in the artist is the seed of a dream growing into a book, a painting, a poem, which awakens in the one beholding it another shadowy dream that, like a reflection in a pool, takes on mysterious shape and substance; and suddenly there is a communion of dream with dream, not on the bright surface but in the secret shadowy places. It may be for only a moment, or for all of a life, but two fantasies have met, magically bridging time and space, and whispered their secrets to each other. This is art's power over us; and its terror, for there are dreams we do not want aroused, ash that must remain ash. And sometimes in fear we turn and rend a poem, a book, a painting, a truth that has blown too steadily on forgotten graves of memories calling forth ghosts whom we have forbidden to walk the earth again. This is also the secret of tradition's hypnotic power over the minds of a region though most of those minds may know tradition only by hearsay.

Southern tradition, segregation, states' rights have soaked up the fears of our people; little private fantasies of childhood have crept there for hiding, unacknowledged arsenals of hate have been stored there, and a loyalty covering up a lack of self-criticism has glazed the words over with sanctity. No wonder the saying of them aloud can stir anxieties until there are times when it seems we have lost our grasp on reality.

Part Three

Giants in the Earth

1

Distance and Darkness

ONLY A MAN or woman who has traveled in childhood the old sand or clay roads of the South in buggy or wagon, who has stayed in the country after nightfall, can know what distance and darkness meant in the making of the rural mind of the South.

Distance was not a word but a force pushing a man hard against his memories and fears, isolating him from a world to which he had never felt securely tied. When the sun set, the night began. There were no lights; only a kerosene lamp or a pine knot burning. And always the swamp back of you or the dark hills, or empty fields stretching on, on. . . . Far off, the Negroes singing in dim lantern-lit churches, moaning their misery and shouting their joy. Sudden sharp laughter from nowhere.

City people, townspeople, have little idea what this meant and still means in parts of the lonely South. During the war they felt the wear on nerves of the blackout, but country folks have lived in a blackout since time began. Darkness comes. Sounds creep out: whippoorwill, tree-frogs, roar of alligator back in the pond, rustle of pal-metto, restless, never-ending, as if an unseen hand brushes over it and it cannot let go . . . the scream of a cat in the swamp. Sounds like these weave in and out of lonely fan-

tasies, pulling in hearsay tales, making a tight mat of facts
and feelings and fancies and fears until one no longer
knows the real from the unreal, and sometimes one no
longer cares. The sweet things too: jessamine crawling on
fences and trees, giving out a wonder of yellow fragrance,
bays blooming white and delicate down in the swamp, and
water lilies fattening on green pond water, making you
love the loneliness you hate, making you want to stay
even as you feel you must leave or die.

Sometimes as you sat there, crazy Miss Sue would walk
down the road giggling to herself. You'd say, "Howdy,
Miss Sue," and she would hurry past breathlessly as if to
keep a late appointment or maybe she would stop, turn,
look at you gently as if you were a childhood dream and
then float away in the dusk. And you would watch her,
bemused, not certain after a moment whether it was Miss
Sue or your own strange notions walking down the road
beyond you.

Sometimes a man sat on the front steps, talking a little
about the crop or the next day's farm work, whittling
on a stick, maybe just thinking, now and then aiming his
spittle to hit the bull's-eye of a totally imaginary spot.
Have you seen that? That is rural adventure, rural fun!
No wonder a man-hunt took on zest, with no more
thought given the running, frightened human being than
to a running, frightened animal. One centered on one's
own excitement. After all, the "best" people of the South,
the leaders, the preachers, the writers, the editors, those
who give value to living, said Negroes were less than
human and were not to be treated as human while alive,
why then did they have to die like humans! Out in the
country, animals do not seem so different from men.
Sometimes they seem closer to you than human beings,
close enough that you want to mate with them, especially
when you are young, and sometimes you do. But animals
are killed to be eaten, or when they get in the way. . . .

Blood-letting is a thing one gets used to in the country.
Hog-killing . . . sticking a pig, hanging it up, listening
to those human-like squeals, watching blood streak the
flesh. . . . Negro-killing. . . . So strangely akin—in sick
minds that hold no words to stop the deed.

(Southern culture has put few words in the mind to
make the difference between human and animal. The
words in the white mind are words that turn the Negro
into animal, words deliberately fed to people to place the
Negro beneath the level of human, to make him not only
animal but a "menace." So much cruelty is on a somatic
level. It is a man's dreams that make him human or in-
human and a man who knows few words to dream with,
who has never heard, in words said aloud, other men's
dreams of human dignity and freedom and tender love,
and brotherhood, who has never heard of man the creator
of truth and beauty, who has never even seen man-made
beauty, but has heard only of man the killer, and words
about sex and "race" which fill him with anger and fear
and lust, and words about himself that make him feel
degraded, or blow him up crazily into paranoid "superiority"—how can he know the meaning of *human!*
How can he know that? Only his own mother's love for
him and his love for her, and his love for his own child,
have given him a conception of human love; that is all
he knows of tenderness; and there have been few words
in his mind to help him transfer this tenderness to other
human beings, few symbols out of which to create
bridges between himself and the rest of the earth's
people.)

Sometimes, when even his mother had not given him
love, and tenderness had been withheld from him and
too much guilt laid on him, and loneliness had lasted too
long and darkness had forced his eyes to turn inward on
sights he could not bear to remember, then something
got into a man. A man hunt then became not an animal-

killing or a fox hunt but a break-through of perverse feelings and deep bitter hatred known in childhood; and when this happened, no cruelty seemed enough to satisfy the hunger that drove men on. Such a man hunt is a journey into all that has been forbidden by religion and by women, a group flight into a strange free land of fury which the rational mind finds hard to understand. It is like the violent murders we read about or have known to happen on our own street: the good man, superintendent of Sunday school, who, one morning at breakfast, turns and shoots down his children, his wife, then himself. Or the girl, sweet, demure, gentle, who walks in one evening and kills her mother, hacking her body to pieces in a terrible fury that has devoured—like cancer devours the healthy body cells—all the sane love-tissue of her spirit. At such times of fury a mere killing is not enough. One is not satisfied that "the enemy" be dead; one must tear up and mutilate until nothing is left to remind one that a person once existed. It is as if one must destroy the very memory of a relationship, tearing every fiber of it out of one's life.

Only a few of our people are killers; only a handful would take a man's life so greedily. But there have been too many lynchings in the South of this nature where the Negro—a stranger to the mob who lynched him—has not only been shot but his body riddled with bullets (each person in the group killing the lifeless body again and again and again), for us not to understand that the lynched Negro becomes *not an object that must die* but a receptacle for every man's dammed-up hate, and a receptacle for every man's forbidden feelings. Sex and hate, cohabiting in the darkness of minds too long, pour out their progeny of cruelty on anything that can serve as a symbol of an unnamed relationship that in his heart each man wants to befoul. That, sometimes, the lynchers do cut off genitals of the lynched and divide them into bits to be distributed to participants as souvenirs is no more than a coda to this composition of hate and guilt and sex and fear, created by our way of life.

No wonder lynchings—however infrequent they are— shock us deeply, for each one is a Sign, not so much of troubled race relations, as of a troubled way of life that threatens to rise up and destroy all the people who live it. And just as one lynching in Dixie shakes the whole world, poised as it is today in such delicate equilibrium, so do the efforts to make lynching a national crime upset on deep unverbalized levels of the mind those southern leaders and their northern associates who gave the privilege of lynching to rural whites as a ritualistic reward for accepting so meekly their design for living, who protected it through the years, and who now dread the withdrawal of this compensation, knowing well that the design will crumble quickly, and not knowing at all what will follow thereafter, either in their region or in their own minds.

Distance and darkness have set the rural South apart from the rest of our nation. Darkness of mind and of countryside. And terrifying ignorance. What good does it do to repeat illiteracy figures to readers whose minds have been nourished well since they were born? How can we who were fed so bountifully feel what it means to live with a mind emptied of words, bereft of ideas and facts, unknowing of books and man-made beauty? It is as difficult as for our well-fed bodies to know the weakness of one who has never had a full meal. To hear that the South's average literacy is fifth or sixth grade, that until the New Deal almost no rural counties had libraries, that few rural families read even the county paper, is not to understand but sometimes only to shield one's mind with facts from realizing such mental emptiness.

Distance and darkness and starvation and ignorance

and malaria ate like vultures on our rural people not for a few Civil War years but for two centuries.

But worse things happened. We cannot forget that these rural people were not let alone. It would have been far better for them had they been ignored, as were most of the peasants of the world until communism's recent efforts; as the southern poor whites were let alone during the days of slavery; and as the mountain whites were largely ignored until the past four or five decades. But the politicians—as is true, today, all over the world—needed the rural people and used them as ruthlessly as Negroes were used when they were needed. They needed to play voter against voter and all of them against "the Negro"—and they needed the poor whites' approval of acts which the dominant group's more informed minds could not wholly approve. They needed poor whites to be their yes-men, moral henchmen quieting their leaders' uneasy consciences. Like David playing on his harp to Saul, the rural whites sang the lies the dominant group wanted to hear, but they were lies that not David but Saul had composed, though Saul never more than half believed them. It was only the poor-white Davids who learned to love these lies which they needed sorely to believe were true. To be "superior," to be the "best people on earth" with the best "system" of making a living, because your sallow skin was white and you were "Anglo-Saxon," made you forget that you were eaten up with malaria and hookworm; made you forget that you lived in a shanty and ate pot-likker and corn bread, and worked long hours for nothing. Nobody could take away from you this whiteness that made you and your way of life "superior." They could take your house, your job, your fun; they could steal your wages, keep you from acquiring knowledge; they could tax your vote or cheat you out of it; they could by arousing your anxieties make you impotent; but they could not strip your white skin off of you. It became the poor white's most precious possession, a "charm" staving off utter dissolution. And in devious, perverse ways it helped maintain his sanity in an insane world, compensating him—as did his church's promise of heaven—for so many spiritual bruises and material deprivations. For though their religion took most of the rural whites' pleasures away from them, dirtying the human body until it was a nasty thing, making dancing and card playing and the drinking of even a glass of beer wrong, thus adding severe strains to bodies already drained by poverty and ill health and loneliness, yet the revivalists did give them reassuring promise of food, raiment, and golden pleasures in heaven, telling them again and again that Jesus died so their souls could be saved after death, from hell; and though they did nothing about starved minds and bodies, nothing about health and jobs, demagogues did keep their starved spirits alive here on earth with the drug of white supremacy and Negro-hate which the revivalists never named as "sins." Listening to words of revivalist and demagogue, the poor white, despite his misery, believed himself important among men, for Jesus had died for him, and his "white blood" made him superior to all other people: "niggers," "furriners," Jews. All you had to do was to "believe" in Jesus and to hate all unbelievers, to be "saved" in heaven; and to "believe" in white supremacy and to hate and shun all who were different, to be "set apart" here on earth as supreme. "Oh, wash me, and I shall be whiter than snow, whiter than snow, yes, whiter than snow," was a song crooned by millions to lull themselves into one vast communal daydream, in order to escape a too-hard reality.

It is impossible to understand these pitiful delusions of grandeur, clung to by millions of impoverished, ignorant, lonely, confused people unless one is willing to look for not "one cause" but a series of causes and effects spiralling back through the centuries.

These people were the rejected of Europe, and feeling their rejection, they rebelled against those forces that had injured them. They were hurt people, "agin the world" that had hurt them; refugees, seeking escape from too-heavy pressures, who came to a warm humid climate where new pressures, new enemies awaited them: malaria, typhoid, wild animals, Indians, loneliness, and a new cultural conflict whose seeds had begun to sprout in 1619 when the first African was taken off a Dutch man-of-war in Virginia. Many of the refugees had lived in the slums of European and English cities and knew little of the land and how to make a living from it. Others (in later decades) fled the potato famine in Ireland. They came to the new country as if to a promised land, eager to "begin again"; not to change themselves, not to understand their past experiences, but simply to "begin again" with the same old selves in a new setting; and a few came to the new country in blind psychic flight moving in the direction which the fresh strong wind of a new age opened up most easily to them.

Most of them had never read a printed page. Few, even of their leaders, were men who possessed educated minds. They had never learned to look at the past or understand it as it had been experienced either by them or their ancestors. Actually, there were few pages of the past clear enough for the most learned to read. Science was only beginning to roll back the fog that covered the universe. Names like Galileo and Copernicus and Descartes and Newton had never been heard by most of these early settlers; the theory of evolution was not a controversy, it was hardly a dream when many of the religious refugees fled English shores. But there was a feeling which most men felt—that knowledge was "wrong" and only faith was "right." The darkness was good because men had always stumbled around in it; ignorance was natural because men had been bruised on it so long; one's belief is more important than what *is*, for one has never known what *is*; one's fantasy is more "real" than reality; the familiar, though it destroy you, is better than the strange, though it heal you. And believing this, they feared the lighting of one candle that might push back the darkness and show what was really there. No wonder they turned away in fear when science began to swing great searchlights across the universe, and to send up hypotheses like flares into the unknown!

And though the winds also blew fine words across the world, of man's importance, of human "rights," that fell like an accolade, singling men out one by one from the anonymous mass, making them blink with the sudden honor awarded them as persons, most of these settlers in the New World reached out only for the words they liked, and of these, *I am as good as you* were the ones their wounded spirits needed.

This fear of scientific knowledge, this leaning on an Authority for a faith to believe in, the rebellious refugees brought with them to America from a Europe still medieval in thought. And as they moved southward along the Appalachian trails into the mountain coves and valleys, or followed the rivers from the southern coast into the rich lands where they built their great farms or their new towns or their lonely little shacks in woods and fields, they clung to the old way of thinking, as if to a part of their body.

Once in the new country, the refugees were cut off from the Europe they both hated and secretly loved, and the clock of European culture stopped ticking for them, its hands fixed on the date of their voyage from the old home to the new.

For often these rebels did not meet one traveler from

Europe in a lifetime, or read one of the new books being written. Nor did many visitors from the city centers of the New World come their way.

In isolation each refugee began to live his life, weaving it of his inner needs and conflicts and dreams and of the new external circumstances as he found them. Those whose energies were free, who could work, who valued money and material possessions, got them by reaching out and exploiting circumstances, accidents, and people to their advantage.

The black man fell into their design and was made the most of. Land was acquired, money saved, more land and slaves purchased, homes built, possessions accumulated, and new powers felt. By the time of the Civil War in 1861, only one-tenth of one per cent of these old refugee families owned as many slaves as did Scarlett O'Hara's family; only two and one-half per cent owned four or more slaves. But 200,000 families out of 5,600,000 whites did own at least one slave and the ownership of one human being as slave is enough to put a Christian's conscience and mind in bondage for a lifetime. For though one slave profits him little yet always he hopes for heavier profits since he has invested so much of his integrity in the system which now he is compelled to defend. And, though eighty per cent did not own even one slave and continued their small living from tilling the soil, or from hunting and trapping or the setting up of shops where the services needed by rural people could be met, many hoped some day to own one and thought of themselves as slave-holding people, identifying in fantasy with the plantation South, especially after their defeat in the Civil War.

Only a people aggressive, wasteful and greedy could have stripped the soil and the forest of richness as did these southern settlers. Taking what they needed from it, then throwing it aside, uncaring what happened to it, was an outward expression, an acting out, too often, of their secret feelings about women. The gullied land of the South, washed-out and eroded, matched the washed-out women of the rural South whose bodies were often used as ruthlessly as was the land; who worked hard as the animals; who submitted to a rough, coarse, furtive love-making knowing nothing else; who bore children in great pain because their culture (and sometimes their church) was uncaring that they suffered; who were often segregated in church (as were the Negroes in old days), sitting on separate pews from the men; who were not thought fit to be citizens and to vote until three decades ago; and who in some states cannot own property except in their husband's name; who, even now, cannot officiate as ministers in most of the churches though they keep the breath of life in them. No wonder a demagogue talking on rural courthouse steps can buy the votes of these malnourished, worn-out, lonely women of the South, with his talk of "sacred womanhood" and "purity" and "protecting our women from the menace of Negroes," for he is buying votes with a dream.

In the early spring of 1948, one of Mississippi's politicians delivered himself of this tribute which reaches a high peak even for southern chivalry:

Now what of the ladies? When God made the Southern woman he summoned His angel messengers and He commanded them to go through all the star-strewn vicissitudes of space and gather all there was of beauty, of brightness and sweetness, of enchantment and glamor, and when they returned and laid the golden harvest at His feet He began in their wondering presence the work of fashioning the Southern girl. He wrought with the golden gleam of the stars, with the changing colors of the rainbow's hues and the pallid silver of the moon. He wrought with the crimson that swooned in the rose's ruby heart, and the snow that gleams on the lily's petal; then, glancing down deep into His own bosom, He took of the love that gleamed there like pearls beneath the sun-kissed waves of a summer sea, and thrilling this love into the form He had fashioned, all heaven veiled its face, for lo, He had wrought the Southern girl. . . .

Listening, many lonely country women who have rarely felt esteemed or beloved, are suddenly caught up by a vision of themselves as Sacred Womanhood on a Pedestal, as Southern Madonnas, and though in a few hours they will be back totin' slops to the pigpen, milking cows, cooking supper, yet for one miraculously sweet breath of time they are transfigured by this image of themselves and they will never forget it. A vote, which is drawing a few lines through names on a piece of paper, is a small thing to give a man who has made you feel revered for the first time in your life.

As time went on, as circumstance piled high on circumstance to make a living easier for the few and harder for the many, large groups of rural southerners grew less inclined to "better themselves," and more effortless in their living. The old pioneer community of interests, the simple rural democracy of men sharing equally in danger and disease and duties was cracking apart. Those who were ambitious continued to collect slaves and more slaves, and more and more land, pushing the others to the edge of the slave system and off the rich land, closer to swamps and hills. Sometimes a man became slave owner not only because of a good headstart given him by greed but by a small or large land grant in the old days from the Crown. It happened too in a family that one son loved money above all else and his brother seemed not to care for it at all. It happened more rarely that a man had a conscience about this matter of slavery while another accepted it as the "right" of the white race. Such separations as these came about in families until after a generation or so, wealthy planters had seedy-looking cousins back in the poor lands, and po' folks could claim to be "blood kin" to the richest folks in the county.

A thousand such accidents—health, temperament, glands, conscience, greed, and luck—like a giant hand pushed the few into great wealth and the many away from it. And though there were those in between, owners of small farms or service shops, and the doctors, lawyers, preachers of the region, a separation began in minds that had already taken place in living: a chasm between rich and poor that washed deeper and deeper as the sweat of more and more slaves poured in it. Those on the other side of the chasm from the large slave owner—and that was most of the South—came to be called "poor whites" and "crackers," "red necks," "hill billies," and "pecker-woods," and a startling lack of sympathy for them slipped into speech and writings and hearts of the planter class.

The few who had profited knew they had sharecropped the people as well as the land and they were made uncomfortable by the knowledge. So they denied Tobacco Road, rubbed it off the maps of their region. And they wrote off the man who lived on Tobacco Road as a liability to democracy for it is his vote that keeps the demagogue in power.

Now, today, they fear him because they helped make him what he is. He has not only been neglected and exploited, he has been fed little except scraps of "skin color" and "white supremacy" as spiritual nourishment. The politicians have dished out most of the racial hog slop but preacher and editor have done their full share, too.

What conception has been given our people of that complex mass of tingling life with its millions of relationships that we call a "human being"? How can we expect them to measure up to today's challenge when they have not been asked to? or have never even heard the challenge defined? Here we are, at the peak of worldwide crisis, when men should be changing their image of themselves and thinking of their survival as moral beings—and what do the leaders say: "Of course we all believe in racial segregation and we'll do everything we can to keep things as they are but we must obey the law." No wonder the words fall like stones on the listeners. This is not addressing man, the proud human being; this is nudging the slave in us, telling it to obey what we do not believe in.

Why shouldn't the listeners feel cheated? They have clung to their white skin when they were jobless and hungry believing it gave them something of value. They have leaned on it as psychic defense. It has become for them, sometimes, more "moral" than law, itself. Now, just as they are moving up the rungs of the old status ladder, with a good job, a car, a television set, the whole thing crashes into a mess of confusion. Somebody doesn't believe what he's saying and they know it. The wonder is that there is not more violence.

But—and here is where things get tangled—the leaders think with sincerity and after much soul searching that they are doing the right thing to withhold insight and fact and to hush up appeals to the ignorant man's ideals and conscience. They do not admit it but many of our leaders do not believe the "poor white" has a conscience nor that he yearns to be good.

So: what happens? Having little moral leadership, when crisis comes—as in Little Rock and New Orleans and elsewhere—the "people" turn to the racists who make their appeal *not* to the conscience but to the mythic mind where the ghosts wander around. And then, the big ghost hunt begins: the hoodlums supported by the racists swing the people into mobs, blow up sputtering feelings into riots, and engage in various forms of secret, anonymous activities.

And we wonder why. We find it difficult to see that not only mobs flourish in a moral vacuum, apathy does, too. The good people who have been speaking out stop speaking. And then we have that strange sickening situation we are getting used to in the South, where 499,000 people sit mute and helpless while a thousand go mobbing and ghost hunting, and a hundred or two hundred of the courageous and the decent risk their lives to stop the rush toward communal destruction.

It need not be.

There are complexities in every racial situation. Never are such matters neat and simple. They can't be. For they reach deep into history, memory, beliefs, values— or into the hollow place where values should be. But the mistake the enlightened leadership of the South (and sometimes, of the North) has made, and is still making in 1961, is to expect people to act wisely without the facts that would convince them of the reason to act, and without belief in the moral quality of their action. They can't do it. We can be swung into war even when our hearts don't go along; but we who are free cannot be driven into a new way of life unless our hearts and minds tell us it is right for us as human beings. A new way of life has to be created. The socalled "racial problem" is not a problem amenable to solution: it is not a problem at all: it is a cruel way of life for which, if we wish to survive as a free nation, a new way of life must be substituted. And such a life requires a new vision, a new grasp of the meaning of the human experience. A new set of values must be found. The Divine Center must be touched, somehow.

As Erich Fromm once said, In the search for God we can only make sure of one thing: that we are not substituting an idol for the Creative Spirit, the I Am That I Am, the Nameless, the Forever Unknown which always eludes comprehension. But an idol—I am paraphrasing Fromm—can be recognized for what it is: something we can name. It may be called *race*, or *success*, or *money*, or *power*, or the *machine*, or *science*. We have our choice: for we are surrounded by crude forms of idolatry. It is not merely the poor and the ignorant who have lost their way.

By stating complexities, one may give an impression that immense difficulties abound in making racial changes. Even though I have stressed the deep-rootedness, the tangled business of reason and mythic mind and memory and the rest of it, I still think our people can change quickly if they are given convincing reasons. There is toughness of mind in Southerners, and tremendous vitality. Most are not sick people nor cruelly perverse; they are starved. Most are conformists rather than idol worshippers. They can be appealed to on a moral level.

Having lived my early life in a Deep South town and much of my recent life in the mountains, I have a bond with rural people which I cherish. The stereotypes built of them by those who are trying to manipulate them, are partly true, of course; but partly false. They do have little learning and can be stubborn as mules; but they have conscience. And they are close to nature and therefore close to the variables of life. They are less aware of large aggregates and samenesses than are urbanites; and more aware of differences and the unpredictability of things that breathe. They are also religious: primitively so, sometimes; but they know and feel deeply the teachings of Jesus. There is also a rough humor, bone-deep. This cannot be disregarded when we are appraising a people's ability to change. I fear the wool-hat boys and girls far less than I do the educated leaders who fear them and therefore desert them in their need—and the demagogic leaders who shoulder the people intimately but exploit them ruthlessly.

As we look across the world, we see the rural people not only of our country but of China and India, Burma, Cuba, Laos, Africa turning like giants in the earth, with their new powers. And we know as we watch that the beliefs they hold will make or destroy our own future.

2

Two Men and a Bargain

BUT SOUTHERNERS did more than exploit, deprive, ignore the poor white, they made a bargain with him. And this bargain I shall tell in the form of a parable, if I may, for it seems the best form for it:

Once upon a time, down South, Mr. Rich White made a bargain with Mr. Poor White. He studied about it a long time before he made it, for it had to be a bargain Mr. Poor White would want to keep forever. It's not easy to make a bargain another man will want to keep forever, and Mr. Rich White knew this. So he looked around for something to put in it that Mr. Poor White would never want to take out.

He looked around . . . and his eyes fell on the Negro. I've got it, he whispered.

He called in Mr. Poor White and said, "I've been thinking a lot about you and me lately—how hard it is for us to make a living down here with no money and the rest of the country against us. To keep my farm and mill going the way I want them to go, making big profit off of little capital, I have to keep wages low, you can see that. It's the only way I can make as much as I want to make as quickly as I want to make it. And folks coming in from the North have to keep wages low too, for that's our southern tradition.

"It's a good way for us rich folks and it's not bad for you either, for you're smart enough to see that any job's better than no job at all. And you know too that whatever's wrong with the South isn't my fault or your fault but is bound to be the Yankee's fault or the fault of those freight rates. . . .

"For instance, the nigger. You don't need *me* to tell you that ever since the damyankee freed him, the nigger's been scrouging you, pushing you off your land, out of your job, jostling you on the sidewalks, all time biggity. If he hadn't been freed, he'd never bothered you, for I could have kept him on the farm and bossed him like I bossed him for 200 years. But the damyankees always know better, don't they! Here I am busy at my mill with no time to boss him, and here he is pushing, causing lot of trouble. Thing I can't forget is your skin's the color of my skin and we're both made in God's image; we're white men and white men can't let a nigger push 'em.

"There're two jobs down here that need doing: Somebody's got to tend to the living, and somebody's got to tend to the nigger. Now, I've learned a few things about making a living you're too no-count to learn (else you'd be making money same way I make it): things about jobs and credit, prices, hours, wages, votes, and so on. But one thing you can learn easy, any white man can, is how to handle the black man. Suppose now you take over the thing you can do and let me take over the thing I can do. You boss the nigger, and I'll boss the money. How about it?

"Anything you want to do to show folks you're boss you're free to do it. You can run the schools and the churches any way you want to. You can make the customs and set the manners and write the laws (long as you don't touch my business). You can throw books out of libraries if you don't like what's in them and you can decide pretty much what kind of learning, if any, you want southern children to have. If science scares you and you don't like the notion of messing around with it, remember you don't have to, this is God's country and a free one. Anyway, it'll tell you things you can't believe and still believe what you believe now so it's better maybe not to take much stock in it.

"If you ever get restless when you don't have a job or your roof leaks, or the children look puny and shoulder blades stick out more than natural, all you need do is remember you're a sight better than the black man. And remember this too: There's nothing so good for folks as to go to church on Sundays. To show you I believe this, I'll build you all the churches down at the mill and on the farm you want—just say the word.

"But if you don't have much to do, and begin to get worried-up inside and mad with folks, and you think it'll make you feel a little better to lynch a nigger occasionally, that's OK by me too; and I'll fix it with the sheriff and the judge and the court and our newspapers so you won't have any trouble afterwards; but *don't expect me to come to the lynching, for I won't be there.*

"Now, if folks are fool enough to forget they're white men, if they forget that, I'm willing to put out plenty money to keep the politicians talking, and I don't mind supporting a real first-class demagogue or two, to say what you want him to say—just so he does what I want about my business. And I promise you: Long as you keep the nigger out of your unions, we'll keep him out of our mills. We'll give you the pick of what jobs there are, and if things get too tight you can take over his jobs also, for any job's better than no job at all. Now that's a bargain. Except, of course, if you're ever crazy enough

to strike or stir up labor legislation, or let the niggers into
your unions, or mess around with the vote, then we'll
have to use the black folks, every goddam one of them
maybe, to teach you a lesson. We'll tell folks—or our
politicians will—that you're mongrelizing the white race
with your unions, we'll tell 'em you're so lowdown you're
begging the nigger to be your social equal, and if that
won't work, we'll tell them the black man is after your
women. We have ways and we'll use them.

"Best thing you can do, seems to me, is to Jim Crow
everything. It'll be easier for us that way to keep the
niggers out of the unions and down on the farm where
they belong, and it ought to make you feel better for a
lot of reasons. For one thing, you can ride with us in
the front of the streetcar and bus and shove the colored
folks plumb onto the back seat. You'll like that and we
won't mind much either—though God knows you can
stink as bad as any of 'em when you go round dirty. But
we'll put up with it, for we don't ride the streetcars and
buses much anyway, and we can see how it makes you
feel a lot better to know you can sit up front and the
black man can't sit there; even if he's a college professor,
he can't sit there, remember! So fix that up any way you
say. And you can do the same about trains and waiting
rooms and toilets and movies and schools and churches
and so on. And you can make rules about restaurants and
hotels too if it'll make you feel better. And I reckon it
will, though you aren't likely ever to go into one of
the hotels or restaurants you put your Jim Crow rule on.
But even if you don't have money to go in one of them,
it'll make you feel good to know you're sort of bossing
things there. . . . So go on and fix all the Jim Crow you
want. When you don't have meat to eat and milk for
the younguns, you can eat Jim Crow and if you don't
think too much about it, you'll never know the difference,
for you don't seem to have much sense, anyway."

And Mr. Rich White and Mr. Poor White thought they'd made a good bargain.

It never occurred to Mr. Rich White that with a bargain the Negro could help him make money. It never occurred to Mr. Poor White that with a bargain the Negro could help him raise wages. For neither ever thought about the Negro as somebody who could help folks make money. Neither ever thought about him as somebody who could make a real bargain. Always the Negro was somebody who took things away, scraps and taxes, prestige, shoddy and second-hand things, but things away from you. Always he was something you had to prove you were better than, and you couldn't prove it, no you couldn't prove it. And always he was something you had to hate and be afraid of. It was sometimes like this: If he wasn't human like you said, if he wasn't, you'd never know what he might do, you couldn't count on him; he might do all the things you had wanted to do or dreamed about doing that you knew were not human, all the kinds of things you know other folks would want to do if they were not human. And sometimes it was like this: If you once let yourself believe he is human, then you'd have to admit you'd done things to him you can't admit you've done to a human. You'd have to know you'd done things that God would send you to hell for doing. . . . And sometimes it was like this: You just hated him. Hated and feared and dreaded him, for you could never forget, there was no way to forget, what you'd done to his women and to those women's children; there was no way of forgetting your dreams of those women. . . . No way of forgetting. . . .

Yes . . . they thought they had a good bargain.

They felt pretty easy about things for a while, for it seemed this would fix anything. They proudly told the world that the South had no Negro problem, it was all settled. They bragged that nobody understood the Negro like the South did, nobody understood the South's business like the South did, nobody understood southern labor like the South did, and the South had fixed things up. Yes, had fixed things up all right for Mr. Rich White and Mr. Poor White and the Negro.

(And Mr. Rich White from the North came South and saw how it worked and went home and told folks about it. Those southerners may be touchy, he said, but they know how to fix things. There's nothing that would help us more up here than to fix things up the way they've fixed them. With the Negroes coming up now in droves, we can do it, if we bring Jim Crow up with them. Thing for us to do is get restrictive covenants started and segregate without putting up signs. Folks up North might be embarrassed about the signs. But if you're smart, you can segregate without signs, and if you get it going, Jews and a lot of other folks can be segregated along with the Negroes. They have a lot of slogans we can use up here too, things like *you can't legislate hate*, and *change comes slowly*, and don't forget the one about your sister. It'll work in the North as well as in the South. As a matter of fact the Republicans would do well to keep the bargain with the Dixie politicians they made in 1876. That's the best way to stop communistic liberals! And the North listened, and it wasn't long before they too began to fix things. . . .)

Down South, folks began keeping their bargain. They began to segregate southern living. They segregated southern money from Mr. Poor White and they segregated southern mores from Mr. Rich White and they segregated southern churches from Christianity, and they segregated southern minds from honest thinking, and they segregated the Negro from everything. And it wasn't long before everybody knew about Jim Crow and talked about Jim Crow and thought about Jim Crow and Jim Crow took on a great importance.

Jim Crow was Mr. Rich White's idea but Mr. Poor White made it work. Mr. Poor White put his mind on it and his time, for he had plenty of time when he didn't have a job, and he made it work. He had ways. Lynching was a good way, and so was flogging. Burning folks' houses was another way. And all these ways eased the feeling he had that he'd lost something, made him almost believe he had found it. . . . And sometimes it eased things in Mr. Rich White's heart also.

But again and again Mr. Rich White's sons and daughters, or his kinfolks or his friends' children who worked for him, or the poor white's children who somehow or other got to college and into good jobs, would forget that Jim Crow is important; and others among them whose hearts refused to go along with southern custom, would try not to practice it; and sometimes a newspaper man who wrote for the rich man would write a brave editorial; and sometimes a preacher who was supported by the rich man would preach about Jesus and love and brotherhood. But not for long. No, not for long. For Mr. Poor White would show them. Mr. Poor White would remind Mr. Rich White of their bargain. Sometimes he did it by coming to the office and talking. But most times he did it more simply by going out and lynching a Negro, or burning a house down, or burning crosses before other folks' houses, or starting a riot, or smearing nasty lies on a man's name until he was sickened to silence. . . .

And Mr. Rich White, seeing these things, would remember. He would remember that Jim Crow is important to everybody. And he'd tell his newspaper man and his preacher and his teacher and his children and the poor white's children who worked for him and all the others that they must remember not to talk about human dignity and love and brotherhood, for talk like that stirs up trouble. They must remember the bargain and hush . . . hush their talking, hush their mind from its questions, hush their hearts from feeling human.

If Mr. Poor White broke the bargain, if he talked too much about unions or tried to organize new unions where there hadn't been unions, or tried to get Negroes into unions, then the other poor whites fixed him. Most times it was Mr. Rich White's idea; sometimes the poor whites'; but they fixed him. They flogged him, or feathered and tarred him, or ran him out of town, or shot him down like you would a hound dog. And they knew they could do it and nothing would happen. They knew they were free to lynch and flog, to burn and threaten each other and nothing would happen, for they had a bargain. They had a bargain with Mr. Rich White and he'd fix the police and the papers and the court and the judge and the jury and the preacher so nothing would happen.

Mr. Poor White felt his power and he used it. He raised hell with Negroes on buses and streetcars and day coaches whenever he felt the need to raise hell. He threw books out of libraries and tore up magazines whenever he didn't like what was in them. And sometimes just because he could not read or write, he had fun tearing them up. He decided when something could or couldn't be taught, whenever he wanted to. He decided on folks' morals: when they could drink liquor and when they couldn't, how they must treat their wives, what they could say about sex and God and science and country and the Negro—and how they could say it; and the manners they could use toward other people. He said when you could and when you couldn't use the word *mister;* when you could and when you couldn't tip your hat to a lady; who could come in your front door and who must go to your back door; who your friends could be and who your friends couldn't be. He told the newspapers what they could say and how they could say it—except about money. (Mr. Rich White told them about money.) He told the preachers what they could preach and how they must preach it—except about money. (Mr. Rich White told them about money.) He told the teachers what they could teach and how they must teach it—except about money. He was boss and he knew it. Boss of the Negro and boss of the white, boss of your home though you might never invite him in it; boss of your church though he might not worship with you; boss of everything in Dixie but the money. Boss of everything but Mr. Rich White's way of making money. Boss of everything but wages and hours and prices and jobs and credit and the vote, and his own living.

Sometimes the newspaper man or the preacher or the professor or the social worker, or a writer, sometimes a group of church women, or his own children, went to Mr. Rich White. "This thing can't go on," they'd say, for they were worried; worried and troubled and dismayed, though it was hard to find words for their feelings. Worried at the poor white's starving and diseased and towering stature; worried when they remembered colored friends, old playmates, and beloved childhood nurses; worried about that poor, frayed word *democracy* which a lot of them still believed in, and heartsick, for some would have liked to be decent and some cherished truth and freedom, and some still hungered to be loyal to the teachings of Jesus, and some knew only that change must come to keep the earth from destruction and must come quickly.

Mostly they called their worry "the Negro problem," and sometimes it was "civil rights" or "the recent lynching" or "the flogging incident" or the Ku Klux Klan or "our school system" or "increasing crime" or "the health of the underprivileged" or "bad housing." And sometimes those more brave talked simply of human dignity and of hungry people, hungry and jobless and homeless and ignorant and bewildered black and white people. But few dared talk against segregation; few dared question the bargain.

All wanting Mr. Rich White to do something. All wanting things to be different, yet afraid to say aloud what they wanted.

Mr. Rich White would listen and smile to hide his own worry. Smile and say easy, if ladies were present, "You've let the Yankee papers upset you. You've let the Communists get you confused. Thing we must remember, folks, is the poor white's feeling. No use to make him mad. No use to do that, is there? You keep talking about calling Negroes 'mister,' using words like that in the papers, you'll make him mighty mad, won't you? You'll make him mad if you say so much about Negro schooling. You'll make him mad talking about equal salaries for colored and white teachers, and higher education. He won't like it. You'll make him mighty mad talking about the white primary for you know he'd rather not vote himself than have Negroes voting. You know that, don't you? You'll make him crazy mad talking about jobs for Negroes, jobs in the mills for colored folks. He doesn't want them working side by side with him. You'll hurt his morale talking about Jim Crow in the army, you can't do it! You got him upset now talking about science books and freedom of thinking. He don't want his children doubting God or thinking too much about anything. I'm not so sure myself but it's science and too much thinking that's wrong with all of us—the whole world, maybe, thinks too much about everything!

"And you can't speak about riots just after they've happened. Maybe when there hasn't been one in a long time, you should say a little something, something about violence being a disgrace, bad, and about the Klan being uncivilized. But not right after there's been an incident in your own town. You'll only stir up trouble if you do it. You got to keep things like that out of the papers.

Thing we got to do, folks, is to keep *everything* out of the papers—except talk against the damyankee's meddling. Way to make things better is for everybody to hush talking."

And after the folks had left, Mr. Rich White would sit a while thinking; then he'd call in his newspaper boys and he'd tell 'em. "Better keep off those problems. Better write a piece about southern tradition. Better write a piece about segregation—that'll please the poor white and kind of calm him down—say it's here and nothing can change it, nothing can change it, nothing, not even Godamighty! Here wait—leave out that about God, just say *nothing can change it!* Better write something against union leaders, be easy on the workers but hard on their leaders. Say something about CIO being nigger-lover and Communist. That's always good. And something against Harlem Negroes and the NAACP. Write something about Yankees meddling with our affairs and something against FEPC and the New Deal and make it plain that human rights are never as important as states' rights, but don't use *human*, think of some other way to say it. Keep saying that whatever is done about race has to be done by the South in its own way. Keep saying that. And be sure to say, 'Nobody but a fool would want to do away with segregation!' Better write plenty about unfair freight rates and the South being a colony of the North and about how wicked a place Harlem is. And wait a minute, boys—write something good about folks needing to read their Bible and go to church on Sunday, folks needing the old-time religion."

Lord yes, Mr. Rich White whispered as he sat there thinking and worrying, got to make 'em know everybody had better keep to his bargain, and everybody better get more religion. A good old-fashioned revival would help us all down here right now. Every one of us.

Sometimes the Negro would tap on Mr. Rich White's back door, ease in, hat in hand, and say howdy. Sometimes he'd tell Mr. Rich White what a fine man his father was and how he is just like him. And then he'd ask a little favor. The favor might be to borrow five dollars, or maybe it would seem just as measly as that when the Negro said it, but it might be about school books for the colored folks, or a new roof on the church or the schoolhouse, or a raise for the teacher, or it might even be about paving a street through Colored Town or fixing a sewer line, or a playground, or a clinic for Negro babies. But way the Negro said it, it'd sound nothing much, and Mr. Rich White would think: It's the least I can do to do it; and he'd say, "I don't see why we can't manage that, Sam, glad you came in to see me." And the Negro would leave, hat in hand, saying, "Thank you, Mr. Rich White, thank you." And nobody would know but the Negro that Mr. Rich White had broken his bargain with Mr. Poor White. Nobody would catch on but the Negro. But the Negro knew. He knew too from three centuries of learning that if you want something from Mr. Rich White or his sons and his daughters you ask it as a favor and not something due you, for Mr. Rich White made his bargain with Mr. Poor White and the white North made a bargain with the white South but nobody's made a bargain with the Negro.

That's right. Nobody made a bargain with the Negro. He just kept on living without one. Kept gnawing the bones from Mr. Rich White's beefsteak, drinking the potlikker from Mr. Poor White's turnip greens, taking Mr. Rich White's favors, wearing his second-hand clothes, picking up the jobs Mr. Poor White threw him, riding the back seat, going in the back door, but going. . . .

And nobody thought anything due him, for the Negro never knew he had a bargain. All he did was keep going . . . singing, dancing, working, lying and stealing, fighting himself . . . and thinking . . . studying about things till he knew them, studying about ways till he found them, making things with his mind and his hand and his heart that the world knew were important, dreaming his dreams . . . and, yes, sometimes bowing, bowing and scraping and laughing, laughing easy at the white man, laughing easy at Mr. Poor White and Mr. Rich White, laughing loud at Mr. Negro, laughing belly laughs at Mr. Negro to hide his sorrow and his fear and his anger and his shame that nothing was due him.

Nobody told him for a long time that up in Washington he still had a bargain. Nobody told him up there were Nine Men who could read it. Had to find that out for himself. Even then . . . even then . . . it's a long way to Washington and it takes money, takes powerful money and time and courage to knock on the door of Nine Judges and ask them to read you your bargain, ask them to read it out loud, so everybody in the world can hear it. . . .

After a time Mr. Poor White got to studying. Seemed like things ought to be kind of different. Mighty fine to sit in the front seat by Mr. Rich White, mighty fine to turn round now and then and see the nigger right there on the back seat where you shoved him. But still, you ain't driving. Mr. Rich White's driving, and you get restless, for it looks like he's driving down a road that goes nowhere, when you need to stop at the store to do some buying. Need to get flour and meat and milk for the younguns and shoes for the family and a new roof over your head and medicine for the baby, and a job that won't wear out tomorrow, and a few games to play with.

But Mr. Rich White says, "Can't stop now, better keep watching that nigger!—Is he still on the back seat, still there where you shoved him?"

"Yeah," you say, "he's still there."

"Well, what's the matter? Don't you like sitting up here on the front seat by me, don't you like that?"

"Yeah, I like that," you say, "but folks got to have things; folks can't keep on making out with what they have forever; seems like I oughta stop at the store and do some buying; seems like maybe you've taken a road that don't stop at stores," Mr. Poor White said suddenly.

"Listen," said Mr. Rich White, "you want me to let that stinking nigger come up here and sit with you? You want that? Want him to marry your sister?" And he slowed down as he said it.

"No," said Mr. Poor White, "reckon that ain't what I want, I couldn't stand that."

"Didn't think you could," said Mr. Rich White, speeding up a little as he drove on down the road that went nowhere.

Mr. Poor White kept studying. Wonder if he *was* up here, could the two of us turn that wheel a little way in my direction?

"I've heard tell," said Mr. Rich White as he drove on to nowhere, "of communist folks and cross-eyed liberals so lowdown they'd associate with niggers just to get 'em into their unions. Ever know a white man low-down as that?"

"No," said Mr. Poor White, "never knowed a white man low-down as that."

"Brother," said the black man in the back seat (easy-like), "don't you think we could do it? Together we could do it?"

"Maybe," said Mr. Poor White (voice mighty easy), "maybe; but you couldn't come near me except in the union, you hear that?"

"Yessir," said the Negro, "I hear that."

The bargain was breaking. Mr. Rich White's and Mr. Poor White's bargain was breaking. Nobody knew how it happened, but they knew it. Breaking in slivers, sloughing in dry rot, and sometimes cracking with a terrible scream as of deep-rooted trees split by lightning.

Folks said it had to break, you ought to see that; times are changing, ways of making money are changing, the world is changing; things can't keep on forever in the old way.

But Mr. Rich White blamed it on the damyankee and the New Deal and the Communist and Mrs. Roosevelt and the Negro press and the social scientists and that little fellow in India and southern traitors and a crazy world that won't stop shrinking, and on his own sons and daughters and their mothers, who didn't seem to know that if you keep talking about the white primary, keep talking about equal education, keep talking about Negro health, keep talking about housing, keep talking about equal jobs and pay, keep talking about fourth-grade sardine-and-cracker culture, keep talking Christian brotherhood, the churches will begin to take brotherhood seriously and Mr. Poor White will begin filling his unions with niggers, keep right on filling them, making them bigger and stronger, and first thing you know he may not even *care* whether he's better than niggers! And then what about money and wages and jobs and hours and things like that! What about the thing you lost long time ago, so long ago you can't remember even what it was, but you keep on hunting it, hunting in your dreams, hunting day and night. . . . Don't they know you got to have *money* to find it! Don't they know things must stay as they are or you'll never find it!

"Let 'em talk," Something whispered. "Long as you have segregation none of these things can happen! Just keep saying *nothing can change it, nothing!* Make your sons and daughters say it and your newspapers say it and your politicians say it. The poor white will say it with you, for he's got to be better than something!"

"You still want to be better than a nigger?" asked Mr. Rich White.

"Yes," said Mr. Poor White, "I still want to be better than a nigger."

"See?" Something said.

"Yes, but why are folks against us! Everybody's against us. . . . The whole world! Even my own children," said Mr. Rich White.

"The southern politician's for you," Something said. "And a lot of Yankee Republicans. And there are people in Europe for you. Plenty folks are still for you. I'm for you—I'm always for the guy who wants to be first; who rides the front seat, always the front seat, and won't let others ride with him."

"Who are you?"

"You know me. Every man knows me until death stops the knowledge. But some won't make me a bargain. You did. Yes. And I'm for you. Who am I? Listen, I'll tell you: I'm that which splits a mind from its reason, that splits a people from humanity. I'm the seed of hate and fear and greed. You are its strange fruit which I feed on . . ."

But Mr. Rich White and Mr. Poor White did not understand the words.

"None but the weak," said a voice, "crave to be better than. Strong men are satisfied with their own strength. There is another way to make bargains . . ."

But Mr. Rich White and Mr. Poor White did not understand the words.

"Must be a Communist talking," said Mr. Rich White, "or somebody un-American."

"Yeah," said Mr. Poor White, "must be some of them folks. What you think, nigger?"

And Mr. Negro said "Yassuh." Then he chuckled, then he began laughing and he laughed and laughed and laughed . . . he just couldn't stop laughing.

"What's the matter with him?" said Mr. Rich White.

"Sounds like he's tickled," said Mr. Poor White.

3

Tobacco Road Is a Long Journey

NO WHITE southerners, rich or poor, ever wrote out this bargain, or said aloud all of it at one time, or faced its full implications, for it grew on them, little by little. They often contradicted it in action, they were inconsistent in expressing it in talk, their conscience made them deny it, their hearts sometimes refused to abide by it. It grew out of bitter years when it was hard for the luckiest man in the devastated South to make a living, out of hurt pride over having lost a war to the Yankee, out of insecurities that reached deep into childhood, out of the aching need for a scapegoat (two were better), out of boredom and an ignorance that made a hodgepodge of ideas, and out of the fact that for the few the bargain paid off in big profits and always one hoped to be one of the few.

It worked for a long time. Each "stood by" the other. When the poor white lynched a Negro, the rich white protected him in court; the preacher protected him in church; the policeman looked away, the sheriff was easily intimidated, the juries rarely convicted, and the newspapers were "reasonable." When unions came South and began to push southern industrialists, the poor white stood by the textile and tobacco mills and fought the unions that had come South to help him gain higher wages and better living conditions; and fought the liberals who were trying to help the rural whites secure better schools and housing and jobs and farms of their own, and hospitals for their sick. It was hard to believe—it is hard today for the rural southerner to believe—that unions are to their advantage; they still are "loyal" to the old bargain, and too, Negro-hating has come now to be such a habit (like the taking of drugs) that many would rather stay poor than give it up; and others hope—those who go to the mills to work—that they can join unions and keep them segregated.

It is equally hard for the rural white to believe that the southern liberals who champion their rights are not "Communists." They call them "Communists" if they fight demagoguery, if they work for higher wages, if they defend human rights, if they oppose war and segregation, if they believe in co-operatives and freedom of conscience and speech which communism does not believe in, and if they fight authoritarianism which communism depends on. The rural white looks with suspicion on southern writers who, loving the South where they were born and live, write honestly of it. It is as irrational as hating a doctor for telling you that you are ill, but many southern whites react in this way, partly because of the bargain and partly because, under the authoritarian system of white supremacy twisted up with Christian fundamentalism, they have been taught to believe one is disloyal when one makes any criticism of things as they are, even when one criticizes great evil.

The political part of the bargain came out of the two groups' conflict with each other during the rise of populism. For a long time the planters had controlled the region's politics. There was the greedy carpetbag interim, the chaotic Reconstruction decade after the war when Yankee and Negro took over for a little; but the Compromise of 1876 eased this sound and fury and the dominant southern group had begun to get things in hand, when out of the Midwest, like a cyclone, came the populist movement—a kind of common-man rural awakening. Southern politics has always bred the opportunism that fattens on what is near at hand; so it was easy for men like Tom Watson of Georgia and Ben Tillman of South Carolina to come forward with demagogic glibness to "befriend" the rural whites. Things began to happen after that. Mr. Rich White's politician voted the Negro en masse to stem the political rise of the "common people"; Mr. Poor White's politician caught on to the trick and voted the Negro himself when he had the power to do so and when he did not, slapped qualifications on law books to keep Negroes from voting at all. In retaliation Mr. Rich White's politician slapped on the poll tax not only to keep the poor white from voting freely but in order to buy up blocs of the poor whites' votes for his own use.

It was more of a battle than a bargain but nowhere was democracy an issue in the fight, as rarely has it been an issue in southern political campaigns since then. Both the Negro and the rural white lost, for the poll tax penalized the poor white man even more than it did the black man (who had already been deprived of the ballot by the grandfather clauses); and the total effect was to take away from both their sovereign right to vote.

The next step was the white primary, which was the means of reconciling the two white groups. After all, using the Negro vote against each other was playing with fire, they said; white folks had better stick together; poor folks and rich both have white skins and cannot afford to fight each other. So they set up the white primary which was in effect an "election," held a few months before general election, in which only white members of the Democratic party—the only real party in the South—voted for the candidates. The white primary was the political bargain by which southern rich and southern poor achieved "peace" and "unity" and made the South solid.

Through its means, not only unity but a political totalitarianism of great power was achieved. It established the one-party system which has made and kept the South solid for seven decades. And, with the aid of the poll tax, reduced voting to a small fraction of the region's citizens of voting age.

But this bargain could never have been carried through had not another bargain been made with the North.

There are a thousand nuances of politics, business, personalities, and prejudice in this agreement known as the Compromise of 1876, but its basic result was to return white supremacy to the South eleven years after the war to free the slaves, in payment for political and economic concessions to the North.

Stripped to its bone the story is this:

After the Civil War when southerners were in panic because of the race disorders of Reconstruction, and northern interests were coveting rich untapped resources of southern materials and markets and labor, and Republican and Democratic parties were in heated controversy over a national election, the Republicans, backed quietly by northern economic powers, agreed to let the southern Democrats manage the "Negro problem" in their own way if their spokesmen would accept the Republican candidate Hayes as President—though there was strong evidence that the Democratic Tilden had actually won the election. The South accepted. Hayes became President, Negroes became the white South's "problem," the Supreme Court drew the teeth from the Civil Rights Act, interpreting the Fourteenth Amendment to accord with this gentlemen's agreement, and suddenly new bright voices in the North began to drown out the old abolitionists' talk of human freedom by saying "the race problem is insoluble."

From 1877 to 1915 there was peace among white folks, North and South. It was not good form to talk of race problems. This white unity swelled into a riptide of stereotyped defenses that made thinking unnecessary. In southern and northern accents the proper answers were said: *The South understands the Negro. . . . After all, the Negro is only three hundred years out of the jungle. . . . Segregation is here to stay; it makes for peace for the races to be separated. . . . You can't change things overnight. . . . This is not the right time. . . . These things have to be done by education. . . . You can't legislate brotherhood. . . . After all, now, would you want your sister. . . .*

The tide of white unity throughout our nation rose higher and did not begin to ebb until the year 1915 brought the Supreme Court's first no to white supremacy in Dixie, in a decision which ruled unconstitutional the voting requirements called "grandfather clauses" (which had been set up in southern states to deprive Negroes of the ballot by requiring proof that their grandfathers had "voted"; in other words, had not been in slavery). But it turned slowly. After one decision, the Supreme Court made no other in favor of civil rights for more than a decade. And, until the New Deal, our national government was loath to break the old bargain.

In the meantime, Negroes had organized in protest against the region-wide discrimination and with the assistance of white friends in the North began a dramatic defense of their legal rights in the courts and in books and papers and forums. Though many northerners stubbornly held to the bargain, repeating rusty clichés that southerners dreamed up, there were others who began to protest this betrayal of democracy; and there were southerners who turned away from the segregation creed they had memorized in babyhood and refused to bow down to it. Questions were asked. Consciences, North and South, grew more uneasy. Old men on the Court died. New ones took their places. Decision after decision of the U.S. Supreme Court in favor of civil rights, books, poems, protest movements, began to melt the deep-freeze in men's minds.

But, in Congress, the gentlemen's agreement held firm. Southern congressmen, elected by a handful of people, with no Negro constituency (until recently), resolutely maintained their collaboration with northern reactionaries in matters of race and labor, though their speech was heavy with invectives against "Yankee interference" which became now a real threat to their bargain. (It is a nice paradox that southern Democrats can maintain this political bargain with northern Republicans only by holding on to a one-party system which keeps the Republican party out of the South. The whole business takes on a fine Alice-in-Wonderland flavor.)

The South has been kept "solid" by this one-party system which depends for its staying power on highly emotional beliefs in states' rights and segregation. Such a one-party system, as we knew before we began to observe its dynamics in Russia, makes it impossible for the people to decide by ballot any major issue for the simple reason that these issues are obscured by the "line." Political campaigns have been, therefore, mainly battles for power between two factions of the same party, neither of which dares deviate from the white-supremacy line.

Sometimes a campaign begins with a "safe" issue such as economy in government, public roads, or freedom of the university system from political restraint, or even some-

times with as "controversial" a matter as the white primary, or the county unit system. Inevitably, in the fight
for votes—whether or not the issue is related to "race"—
the candidate closest to the rural people will use the
"Negro question" as weapon, plunging it into his opponent by accusing him of being in favor of "social equality." The farcical battle begins. In reply, his opponent
will declare in righteous indignation that he too believes
in segregation, he too believes in states' rights, he too is
as loyal as any son of the Confederacy to southern tradition. But sometimes, if he is a decent person, he will add
that he does want the Negro to have justice. That gives
the heckling candidate the advantage, and now he re-
doubles his accusations until the air is full of incredible
phrases about "menace," "our white women," "enforced
intimate relations," "integration of the races," and so on.
The original issue that might have given the electorate a
small basis on which to make a rational choice, is now forgotten. In an atmosphere highly charged, the people go
to the ballot boxes and vote for the man who is most able
to protect them from the "danger" he has created by his
words.

The accused candidate—no matter how liberal he is in
private—is faced, in such an issue, with only two alterna-
tives which he and his advisers will consider: one is to
meet the accusations in dignified silence; the other is to
reaffirm his loyalty to southern tradition, to repeat and
keep repeating the creed of segregation and thus try to
convince the electorate that he is as ardent a white su-
premacist as his opponent. Neither works well with the
people, for he is on the defensive and a man on the defensive does not cut a fine figure with country folks.
Secretly they are also ashamed that he is unwilling to
come out and take a stand for what is right. They know
in their hearts that this question of human rights is far
more important, far more basic, far more "rational" than

the issue of roads or economy and so on. Were he to turn round and really fight, were he to declare in words of honest eloquence his belief in human rights, were he to make a tight case against segregation that would appeal to reason and also light a candle in men's murky imaginations, he would swing the decent voters in the state to his side. But the politicians in a southern state will not gamble on there being a majority of decent people, and this third alternative is never tried. With profound cynicism they play the game as if no one can be elected in Dixie on a democratic, decent platform.

In my lifetime, there has never been a campaign in the South where a major candidate took a stand against segregation.

It is not only the bargaining away of one's integrity in order to be "useful" that disturbs me about political campaigns, it is the liberals' forfeiture of their opportunity to carry to the people our democratic beliefs. The people are listening as they never listen at other times, minds are ready to receive and ponder what their candidates have to say. The southern conscience, so long deprived of nourishment, is hungry for words that recreate the dream of the importance of the free human being.

But what do our people hear?

In one campaign, not many years ago, they heard this:

White-Supremacy Candidate: As long as I am your Governor the Jim Crow law will be preserved. As long as I am your Governor no Negro foreman will give orders to white men and women in the mills of this state.

Liberal Candidate: If a nigger ever tried to get into a white school in my part of the state, the sun would never set on his head. And we wouldn't be running to the Governor or the State Guard to get things done, either.

White-Supremacy Candidate: For my part, I am proud to be called the champion of White Supremacy.

Liberal Candidate: This state is governed by white people and always will be governed by white people.

White-Supremacy Candidate: Sure . . . the nigger has a place. And that place is at the back door. There's no other place for him.

Liberal Candidate: There is not a decent white man or woman in our state who believes in educating whites and Negroes in the same schools. There is not a decent white man or woman here who believes in social equality among white and blacks.

And when this campaign was over, the Negro and the white man were still in the South, and both were bruised and burnt to the bone by racial hate and fear.

Who is going to stop it, as long as the southerners in politics feel compelled to deny their real beliefs, and newspaper editors feel a terrible necessity to call "fools" and "fanatics" those who take a stand against segregation? Every honest politician, every honest editor, is troubled by this moral dilemma. He knows in his heart there are times when he surrenders his integrity to southern tradition in as bending a way as a Russian surrenders his integrity to the Politburo. And he apologizes for it in the same way a Communist does by saying that ends justify means, that there is no other way to "be useful to the South" except by betraying one's deepest beliefs. And he turns bitterly on "idealists" who question his "realism."

Southern tradition may be only a ghost stalking our land, while the Politburo is a police authority with live guns, but both have the power to take from men their freedom to do right.

It is hard to decide which is more harmful to men's morals, the "moderate" or reactionary, in this confused South.

The reactionary candidate, while not disturbed by a spiritual conflict, having killed his dream so long ago he cannot remember having possessed it, rarely hates or fears

Negroes; yet without one scruple he will plan a campaign to arouse the race-sex anxieties of the whites. In speeches and writings he will deliberately dehumanize the Negro race, deliberately play up sexual fears, deliberately wear down the poor white's belief in human decency until, released from the constraint of conscience by the hysteria which the demagogue has incited, these confused people will do violent acts against any individual or group who is different from them, having been taught that any one "different" is their mortal enemy. After many gubernatorial campaigns in the South, we have a wave of cross burnings and terroristic activities—not because of the few who dare to affirm human rights and dignity and brotherhood, but because of the millions who deny these truths by their silence while race-bigotry and white-supremacy words are chanted over radio and television and in newspaper, day after day. Newspapers are so confused that even the more liberal among them actually believe a denunciation of segregation will "incite violence" and insist that affirmations of human rights can "only do harm." They seem to have forgot that words can arouse a conscience as well as baser passions, and that conscience in sane people is a determining factor in behavior; instead they treat the southern public as if it were either a moral moron or mentally ill.

After the poll tax and white primary laws were passed in the days of our fathers the rest of the Jim Crow statutes were put quickly on the states' law books. Beginning in 1890, most of them were passed in less than two decades. White and Colored signs went up over doors and stayed there. Railroad stations, rest rooms, drinking fountains were labelled. A South mushroomed in strange duality; a sin and its shadow crept over the land. White church —colored church; white school—colored school; white toilet—colored toilet; white waiting room—colored waiting room. In this region of bleak want and poverty, the cost of maintaining white civilization mounted higher and higher though costs were not doubled. No: for Mississippi spent annually on education for the white child in 1945–46, $75.19, for the colored child $14.74; Georgia spent $82.57 for white, $31.14 for colored; South Carolina spent $100.38 for white and $39.64 for colored.

From 1890 on, *white-colored-white-colored* grew into a regional chant that swells when tensions come, diminishes when tensions go, but there is always chanting. . . . Minds and hearts were aroused by political greed, and sadistic fantasies that spiralled higher and higher. Almost anything could happen and much did. The Atlanta riot in 1906 . . . more and more lynchings of more and more sadistic nature, more white women succumbing to fantasies that they had been raped and sometimes there were actual rapings . . . more rumors and gruesome tales of brutality. Although 3,148 lynchings took place in the South from 1882 to 1946, no member of a lynch mob was given a death sentence or life imprisonment. Only 135 persons in the entire United States (according to records of years 1900–1946, during which time almost 3,000 lynchings took place) have been convicted of being members of lynch mobs.

The responsible, educated, well-to-do group who thought of themselves as dominant (or hoped they were) did not know how to stop this monster created of poverty, fear, ignorance, guilt, political greed, and crazed by the drug of white supremacy. Nor could they confess their big role in creating it. So they turned away and laid down a smoke screen of silence over the South's racial tensions. It became taboo to talk of these problems; bad form to question; "irresponsible" to discuss the issues in newspapers or write about them in books. They hoped silence would cure what intelligence and good will felt helpless to combat. If one did not mention these ghosts, maybe they would just go away. If everyone would only tiptoe . . . and whisper . . . and not talk aloud about freedom and dignity and rights, maybe you could keep from stirring up violence. If segregation were never mentioned, just accepted as unchangeable—like volcanoes and hurricanes and droughts—maybe everybody, even the Negro, would finally bow down before it. If we'll all be very quiet, maybe some day we shall wake up and find this hell we are living in is only a bad dream.

I suppose this state of mind—which has begun to change even though revived by each political campaign—was a massive schizophrenic withdrawal before trouble too immense to accept. I remember, as a child, hearing relatives and friends say there was no Negro problem, it was all settled. I remember that, like *sex*, the word *segregation* was not mentioned in the best circles. Everything was shut away. If one came in contact with a Negro one knew, one was courteous, smiling, a bit condescending— as grown folks often are to children. That is all. One's mind refused all questions. Everything was insoluble; therefore everything was settled.

By 1908, most southern states had the movements and habits of their people well covered by laws that made rigid the avoidance customs which had appeared here and there.

Jim Crow was a political trick in the beginning, but a trick that fitted like a glove on the white South's greedy, guilty hand. It paid politicians and still pays them the highest profits they receive in this country. But it paid men even more in economic power—North and South— for it gave them irrational weapon by which to weaken labor and to control politicians who in turn control the rural votes, though the law of diminishing returns has set in concerning its use, and many shrewd industrialists realize it. But these laws paid most profitably of all in closing off the conscience. They hid so much. They justified so much. And gave troubled people the final answer, "You can't break a law, can you?"

People said it and sighed in relief for the state had now decided what their own Christian conscience, for decades, had been unwilling to decide.

This was the "reconciliation" between northern reactionaries and their southern fellow travelers; this was the "unity" in Congress—acclaimed so loudly—when men without integrity made deals that were profitable to both northern and southern economic and political interests and highly unprofitable for American democracy. And this was the beginning of an authoritarian regime in the South during which state, church, home, school, and courts taught or defended the ideology of white supremacy and the constellation of skin-color-purity concepts that fixed and supported it and kept the mind of the people from questioning its "truth." Thus segregation became the South's highest law.

The national Compromise of 1876, the bargain the North made with the South, is a part of the same old story. The South bargained away its economic resources to the North and the North bargained away its rightful share of power in Congress to the South through the poll tax and white primary which its compromise helped bring about. These two ballot restrictions made it possible for southern congressmen to be elected sometimes by as little as five per cent of the potential voters of their districts; and once elected, they can stay securely in Congress, term after term, until seniority bequeaths them the most influential and powerful offices in Senate and House. Today, these southerners, by means of filibuster and compromise with Republican reactionaries, are making decisions affecting not only American lives but the future of the whole world.

Tobacco Road is a long journey . . . leading from eroded little cotton and corn and tobacco patches through the South to Washington, on to Wall Street, to Africa, to India and China, to the days of medievalism and back again to slavery, to state capitals, to Main Street, to Moscow, to ballot box, to the bank, to church and courthouse, to a man's childhood and his deepest fears . . . curving and twisting from one to another endlessly.

4

Southern Waste

WE HAVE STAYED on Tobacco Road a long time because for decades most of our people lived there.

But there were some who could read and write, and a few in every town who went to college, and there were always a handful who loved books and ideas and poetry; and two or three who dared to question and to irritate by their laughter; and sometimes one, maybe two, who wrote or painted or had a serious interest in music.

But bad health and isolation took a heavy toll from our people, and there were few outlets for energy, few ways of salvaging fantasies in word or paint, sculpture or music or dance or in scientific inquiry.

The rigors of pioneer life had much to do with this impoverishment. In early rural society no one owned a "picture" or "statue," rarely a book unless he were of the small wealthy group. There were no art galleries, no public libraries, and little serious music. There was no knowledge of these things, nor money to buy them with, nor time for creating them, for hands and minds were needed for another purpose. They were needed to chop down trees, fight wild animals, break a trail through a swamp, outwit Indians, build houses, open up fields; and this work satisfied most men's psychic needs.

In such a culture, the boy who withdrew with a chunk of clay and a dream and fashioned them into a piece of sculpture, or messed around painting or writing stories, was called a plain fool. Dimly folks sensed, too, that his creative needs were stronger than theirs, that things were happening in him that "decent folks should be ashamed of" and they were ashamed of him—in the same way they were ashamed of the insane member of the family or the daughter who became pregnant outside of marriage.

It was not strange for them to believe in the immorality of the creative process, for their preachers—from circuit-rider to revivalist—had warned them that art, dancing, novels, and curiosity pandered to the evil in men's natures. Critical intelligence was "wrong"—both Catholic and Protestant churches had long opposed the new learning; science was "wrong"; curiosity, already dulled by the suppression of the child's explorations of his small world, was "wrong."

The frustration or guilt that resulted from these restrictions sometimes put a spell on hands and mind so that they could not again connect with daydreams out of which art comes, or with those first questions of the child that are the seeds of mature inquiry. And once locked up, it was not easy to free them again.

A heavy pall had fallen across spirits; so many brightnesses of life were banned; so many easements forbidden. In my childhood, the wearing of jewelry was opposed by many Methodist ministers who quoted the Discipline rebukingly to those of their congregation who prized what they called "sinful baubles." "Painting of the face" and lipstick were frowned upon. "Drinking" is still a greater sin in many religious southerners' minds than segregation, which is rarely thought of as a sin by these strict people. Just as a patient, suffering from melancholia, refuses to "look pretty" or to wear becoming clothes or spend money for pleasure or do anything that might be fun because he "doesn't deserve it," rural and small-town people seemed to feel they must not permit themselves any pleasures but eating—as if in deep penance for a more cherished sin which they could not give up or had committed so long ago they could not remember it. And not wanting to remember, it was wise not to question one's self too closely.

There is much that reminds one of mental illness in this catalog of sins. It was so compulsive, so without humor. When we remember that our forefathers accepted slavery and that our people now accept gross racial discrimination and acute poverty and disease without letting these evils enter the region of "right" and "wrong," it becomes apparent that the morals of the South have been for many only a compulsive cleansing of hands.

Aggression, when not expended against the family, was accepted by this troubled conscience. Wasting of land, wasting of natural resources, lawbreaking, vigilante groups, bootlegging of whiskey in prohibition counties, group violence, fist-fights, became southern characteristics. This acceptance of violence has piled up statistics which tell us that the southern region has proportionately the most murders, as well as the most churches, the most poverty, the highest rate of illiteracy, lowest wages, poorest health, most eroded soil of any section of our nation.

As skilled use of the hands in aggression became more and more valued in this pioneer-planter culture, skilled use of the hands in work was increasingly looked down upon. Men who worked with their hands were depersonalized in this rural region of poverty, where only the white-collar workers were esteemed and especially the professional man and the man who did not work at all. You paid off the "hands," white and black, on Saturday; you put the "hands" to work on Monday morning.

I have sometimes thought that the Southerner's fear of unions springs not alone from his fear of giving up his individualism, but from the fear that if one joins the union and becomes identified with "labor," one will surrender one's chance of becoming a "gentleman" who no longer needs to work with his hands.

Of the varied manifestations of stress in our culture, the fear of hands used creatively and the acceptance of hands that destroy seem to me most revealing. Men grew afraid of their own human stature and of that which contributed so much to creating it.

The colonials of Maryland, Virginia, and the Carolinas, who in early days set cultural levels which the more crude and exploitative planter of the Deep South tried to identify with, placed little more value on the artist and the creative process than did the pioneer and "poor white" and lower-South Methodist and Baptist.

Though they hung many paintings—usually their own family's portraits—in their drawing rooms, this upper-South aristocracy valued the esthete rather than the creator, taste rather than truth, erudition rather than critical intelligence. The creative process was neither intuitively cherished as an emotional safety valve nor prized as the means of symbolizing men's important feelings about life. They, too, with all their surface sophistication, feared their fantasy life as much as did po' folks. The dread of the mythic mind is no respecter of classes and—as is the way of the Anglo-Saxon—nearly everyone preferred to keep a safe distance from the profound depths of his own or another's nature.

But beautiful *things* were valued. Portraits in oils; furniture made by fine cabinetmakers; spinets and crystal chandeliers from Europe; rugs from France and the Near East; china, silver, old vases and clocks from England and the Orient; and hooked rugs of the Piedmont region, found their way during the 18th and early 19th centuries into tideriver homes stretching from Virginia to South Carolina to New Orleans and up the river to the more fabulously elegant homes in the delta. And today, these Colonial and pre-Civil War possessions are esteemed so highly as symbols of a way of life which the few lived with grace and the many identify with, that a number of old southern homes are maintained, like mausoleums, and opened at stated intervals for the devout to visit. These pilgrimages seem to pay those who organize them, and the pilgrims (from North and South) seem to receive commensurate returns if one can judge by their dreamy-eyed stares at all this antebellum grandeur.

As cotton slipped across the land, as slaveholdings grew larger and the rich black fields of the lower South opened up, and a new kind of pioneering took hold of minds, men became too poor or too rich, too tired or too greedy, to develop the resources of their own intellect and spirit. The culture brought over from England to the tideland edges of the South never flowered as in New England but wilted and finally shriveled. So that at the time of the Civil War, there were fine possessions but no art in the South; a few libraries but no critics and writers, a little tinkly music but no composers of importance. Planter families were riding to hounds, drinking mint juleps and dancing, and hotly arguing states' rights and their moral right to hold human beings in slavery. Such a mood was not conducive to reading, but those who, in spite of it all, loved books were reading the Greek and Latin classics, committing to memory Horace and Ovid, holding to these ancient writers as if to a crumbling shore, unable to explore the deeps of their contemporary world, unwilling to make contact with it. And the poorer families were spelling out the war posters which were recruiting soldiers for the new Confederacy.

After the war, the rich who survived, either as the old planter who held on or the new planter who took over, lived much as before, though for a time more frugally. Their sons spent winters in Paris and Italy, a few turned into bookworms as had their uncles or fathers, reading and re-reading the classics, thinking themselves learned because minds blotted up easily words which long ago were torn in anguish or wisdom from another's heart and intelligence. And, here and there, youngsters with more vitality and curiosity turned to southern journalism, hoping to find there what they hungered for. But most of the South during those hard decades was not reading at all. Those who read casually, turned away from everything that did not give them comfort; for evil things were happening in Dixie and most southerners wanted to believe—they *had* to believe—that this evil was not of their making. Only books that convinced them of their blamelessness for the blackness of their times were acceptable.

In nearly two hundred years of white southern culture there was not one artist or critic or poet or dramatist or musician or writer (if we except Poe) produced here who was comparable to his contemporaries in Europe. Only in the past three decades have we had novelists of more than minor worth. Even now, much of our best talent goes into what F. L. Lucas calls "stained-glass writing," which shuts out the glare of the turmoil in man's soul and his world, seducing the mind with its wondrous patterns of words that block off insight carefully and graciously.

Writers became too subdued by the white Christian supremacy system, too overwhelmed by its luxury and poverty, to write of life as they saw it around them and people as they knew them to be. And sometimes, alas, they no longer could see, having closed their eyes. Instead, in devotion or despair, they wrote down the official daydream that the southern authoritarian system wanted the world to think our life was. This conspiracy of blindness, this collaboration with authority, entered into voluntarily but later made obligatory by custom, closed a heavy door on the mind and the senses. People knew so much that they dared not speak of. They realized intuitively so much that they could not convince even themselves was the truth. They dreamed so many dreams that they knew, if written or put in color or clay, would seem to the people they loved to be terrifying nightmares, and to "all the others" an act of treason. Few, almost none, were willing to undergo the public abuse and social rejection that followed disloyalty to southern tradition. (There was in the South no regional or state government with the power to banish such an artist or critic but there were —there still are—gentlemen's agreements and newspapers and the Klan who could make life not worth the living.) Horace Kallen's depiction, in *Art and Freedom*, of the artist as one who maintains his right to be different, carrying gaily and gallantly the banners of freedom down through the centuries, reserving always the right to stay in bondage to his own daydreams and not those of any power or tradition or state, is an artist that the South rarely saw until the last few years.

Our southern artist was more likely, in the old days, to be a lady embroidering a pin cushion or painting flowers on velvet. Our poets were sometimes gentle souls like Lanier, but rarely did one of them put other than his carefully self-censored thoughts on paper, sifting them through layers of taboos and proprieties and decorums. Little appeared in print that could not be read as an inspirational thought at family prayers which many southerners had each morning.

The few who dared mess around in public with paints were usually looked upon as "abnormal"—effeminate if men, lesbian if women. The men of science (evolutionists) were treated with a bit more respect by being called "anti-Christ," while psychoanalysts and social scientists were named "Communists." A boy who was a pianist had to endure the worst treatment of all, being called "sissy" and whispered of as a "hermaphrodite," and was so terrorized by tongues that few survived the ordeal without mental breakdown. And this continued until the day of jazz orchestras and popular band leaders who, whatever their musical achievements, made life more bearable for men musicians in Dixie.

Feelings and attitudes are changing. Artists and writers are beginning to create their own dreams. Critics are beginning to speak their real beliefs, though they still find it rough going among the homefolks.

It is one of many paradoxes of our way of life that among the dominant free, talent was so bound by anxiety that it could not be released, while among the slaves and the segregated, talent burst forth spontaneously.

Though this talent found varied outlets in the work of the artisan, the creative activities of Negroes were for a long time limited to what could be done with their bodies for that was all they had to do with.

Their songs and dance, their spirituals and their jazz, were welcomed by all people of the Western world as hungrily as an undernourished child eats candy. For these creations, this poignancy of song, this access to sorrow and abandon to instinctual rhythms, met a deeper need than most realized, reuniting us with a part of ourselves so long hidden away in shame.

But we wanted none of the Negro's brains. We rejected the intellectual richness that piled high in the minds of those who acquired learning. Negro scientists, and scholars in the fields of law, history, and medicine we tried to ignore. And back of them the long procession of young trained minds we would not look at. Instead,

we shut this wealth away on the campuses of Negro colleges which most southerners have never visited and many
do not know exist.

There are fine buildings, there are beautiful grounds,
and good libraries; there are as well-trained faculties as
in most white southern colleges, and the young people
in them are healthy and eager and perhaps of a higher
intelligence level than the average in white schools; but
there is, even so, something about a segregated college
that reminds me too much of a mental hospital, for the
people inside are shut away from communication with
the rest of America's people—not because they are ill,
but because the culture outside has lost its health.

I remember, once, when I was on such a campus. The
young secretary of the president of the college was showing me the grounds. She was a lovely thing to look at,
quiet, poised, and I found her face more interesting than
buildings and spacious gardens. We walked near the entrance that led to the street and stood, watching a streetcar pass by toward the "white" section of town. And
then we turned back toward the library. I said, "It is
beautiful in here, peaceful, quiet. I find it hard to remember the world out there that I will go back to tomorrow."
She did not answer for a moment, then she said softly,
"I wish I never had to go out there, even to shop. I would
like never to go. In here, one forgets; you can believe
you are real, a person. You go out there and they tear it
off you, your belief in yourself as something good, they
tear it off in five minutes. It doesn't take much, a word
you hear a man say, a glance, some one draws aside, that
is all; a clerk in a store asks you your first * name as if
she cannot otherwise sell you a pair of shoes. Little things.

* This is changing now. Most southern stores value their Negro
patrons, for there is money now in the Negro community. Only
at lunch counters is discrimination common—and this, due to the
students' sit-ins, is changing rapidly.—Author's note, 1961.

. . . And suddenly you are an untouchable. In here . . .
sometimes for a month I do not remember those people,
outside."

In these schools are faculties made up in large part of
brilliant, sensitive, talented, Negro men and women, many
of whom possess the highest kind of scholastic and scientific training. Sometimes a fine white scholar, like Dr.
Robert Park, who was at Fisk University for so long, will
be found in a department. Nearly always, there is a scat-
tering of white missionaries who with good motives and
sometimes good brains, have dedicated their lives to the
"betterment" of the Negro race.

Of these latter, a heavy price is exacted by the white
community for their missionary zeal. Though the attitude is now changing, these white teachers, many from
the North, a few of the South, have been outcasts in the
southern communities. I have been told by them that they
have lived on the campus of a Negro college for twenty
years without receiving a social invitation from the white
Christian community. Yet these same communities send
missionaries to China and India and Africa to save the
"heathen," and graciously entertain these missionaries
(even the ones who have been to Africa) upon their return. It is a thing to ponder. Africa . . . full of white
Americans who in their hearts wanted to do something
to help the Negro in the South and dared not, and turned
instead to foreign missions, finding it easier to brave distance and disease, tropical heat, jungle, plains, loneliness,
than to brave the hostility of their own people. And yet,
even in the missions the prejudice lingers, and sometimes
becomes more tenacious than at home.

In 1947, a young missionary wrote me this letter:

I wanted to stay in the South and help rid it of lynching
and segregation. That is what I really wanted to do. But there
was Mother . . . you know how disgraced she would have
felt had I stayed and helped here. She would have died if
she had seen me eating with a Negro. . . . But she is proud

of me now, going to Africa as a missionary. She calls me her "missionary daughter" and gave a party last week in honor of my going. Mother's friends said they were proud of me too—going so far away to help Christianize Africa. And the president of the U.D.C. in our town is giving me a party next week; she's proud of me too. I am the only one ashamed.

Tonight I feel like a coward for I know I am needed here. My boat sails in two weeks. Maybe in some way over there I can show a little courage. I don't think I'm afraid for my-self . . . it's Mother. I love her; I can't hurt her. How do you learn to hurt the people you love, even when you know they're wrong, for something you know is right? That is so hard.

Yes, it is so hard. And it is a hard thing too that the South has wasted this fine moral fervor by forcing it out of our region, saying there is no room for it here.

Of the Negro colleges, each campus is a little different: the warmth of a generous personality, the releasing effect of one man with a big sense of humor, the bruising power of one man's profound skepticism, the illuminating glow from one giant imagination, the poison freed by one man's deep hate—such intangibles change the atmosphere of a campus, even from year to year, making it impossible to talk as if Negro colleges in the South are alike. But all of them are alike in that their students and their faculties are cut off from the main-stream of American society; and all are alike in that the human beings in them feel psychologically shunned by the rest of America; and all have the certainty that whenever their graduates leave their "retreat," they will be thrust out into a hostile so-ciety that will have doors for them to walk through and buildings that they must keep out of, libraries that they cannot use, research departments in schools of higher education closed to them; and few positions for which they will be eligible because of their color.

Perhaps the wasting away of our people's talents and skills has been the South's greatest loss.

Part Four

The Dream and Its Killers

1

Man Against the Human Being

IT HAS BEEN a sorrowful story I have told here, made of pages out of history and memories of childhood.

But there have also been triumphs. Too much was good and sane and creative in us for our appointment in Samarra to be kept. And finally we turned back toward reality.

It was not an easy journey to make for we had lived in our never-never land so long; we had worn our invisible crinoline skirts with such charm; we had rested our powers of observation so comfortably behind white columns that had crumbled or never been built; we had wandered down grand magnolia-shadowed driveways where only chinaberry trees had grown; we had ridden to hounds though most did not own a mule to plow with; all of us, even those who had shoveled in grits and fatback with a tin spoon, had eaten wondrous southern cooking out of old buried silver the Yankees had stolen. Our life had been, as politicians reassured us during the depression, the "best life anyone has ever lived on this earth." And the *Textile Bulletin* of Charlotte, N.C. reaffirmed this good fortune, stating ". . . nowhere do the yellow race or black race live upon a higher plane than the lowest divisions of the white race."

For people used to such mythic grandeur a return to plain facts was hard. But though we were stunned at the notion of men testing with their senses and technics these matters our wishful logic had proved with no testing at all, that unknown southern region, Reality, was growing clearer each day. Fact piled on fact, and still the social scientists kept at it. There seemed nothing too sacred to listen to, nothing too small to be measured and counted and compared and touched and looked at: churches, mill town, the soil, the shanties, the schools, crops, incomes— when would the fact finders hush!

They didn't. They not only collected the facts about us, they told the world. And we heard, too, and let out some powerful rebel yells. Resistance piled as high as the facts: opposition grew not only to specific facts but to the process of fact-finding. A fact-finder, the political candidate would declare, is a subversive, maybe a spy for Russia. Don't trust anybody caught with a fact! And he would go, this demagogue, from courthouse to auditorium to church box-suppers begging his poor open-mouthed, sagged-down audiences to keep on believing sharecropping and poverty and ill health and moral degradation were fine. He urged them to defend their peonage to a way of life which had eroded land and culture and their own minds. "Remember your old daddy, what was good enough for him is good enough for you, ain't it?" And they'd yell back, "Yeah . . . couldn't be better!" And come September and the white primary, they'd wave the Confederate flag and give him the election.

The preachers stood by, intoning pious defenses of old evils which they masked as our "way of life," and telling everybody what folks needed was to go to church on Sun-

day. And newspapers brought up the rearguard with eloquent editorials, defending almost anything if somebody's
grandpa had done it. Those were the balmy days of the
Mighty Defense of All That Is Wrong With Us. And
somehow, it comforted people to whom *change* was the
dirtiest word in the southern vocabulary.

Wild oscillations swung us back and forth. The New
Deal, first a clever political phrase, then a courageous
encounter with things as they are, gradually became a
symbol affecting literate and illiterate. Some of us clung
to it, half-hypnotized; as it moved forward, we moved.
A few began to read the books that told them about their
own farms, their lack of markets, their lack of industry,
their lack of modern agricultural methods, their lack of
schools and library facilities—and as they read, new possibilities opened before them. Some went in groups to take
a look at the waste and misery they had lived close to
all their lives but had never seen before.

They took a giant step by asking each other: *What is
wrong with our way of life?*
A giant step: then two or three rapid ones—then we
slowed down, turned back toward what we were leaving,
hesitated, went forward again; hesitated, turned back.
One voice could push us on or pull us back; one Fireside
talk, the sound of FDR's warm laughter, could quicken
us; one first-class outburst by a demagogue threatening
us with the old psychotic phrases could paralyze us.

We seemed to have no moral or spiritual protection
against the anxiety which the politician's stereotyped
phrases could arouse. *Sacred way of life* put us on our
knees in idol worship; *rivers of blood flowing* accelerated
our pulses and secret desires; *the nigger is only three hundred years from savagery* blinded us to our own sadistic,
primitive acts. *Outside interference* became a compulsive
cry to every suggestion of change. Always the Outsider
did the evil. There was meaning in this phrase, more than

the speakers knew. For everything that could not live in our mythic minds was Outside. We alienated reason; made strangers of knowledge and facts; labeled as "intruder" all moral responsibility for our acts. Home was the mythic mind—it still is for millions. Here in the mythic mind we could forget time and space, cause and effect; here everything could melt and merge, here we could take one quality, the color of the skin, and make a universe of it. The technics and skills of the reason belonged to the Outside, as did compassion and mercy, as did God. Christian teachings were pushed to the Outside where only Yankees and Communists and "troublemakers" live. The most suspected of all Outsiders was our own future.

There were individuals, a rather large number of them, who managed a fairly good relationship with their reason as long as they could keep off the subject of the South and the Negro and their own whiteness but once these were mentioned, even the more balanced citizens sometimes succumbed to mob thinking although they never joined the mob in the street.

This collective madness—and it is that—which feeds on half-lies and quarter-truths and dread can possess a whole town—as happened in the late '50's in Georgia. It can possess a section of the city, as it recently did in New Orleans; * it can possess a bus station as it did in three cities in Alabama; * or a Governor's Mansion in Louisiana and Arkansas—or a church as in Montgomery.** And during the fiesta of hate and color-lust no appeal can be made. Why? Because there is in many people no Divine Center to appeal to: there is only emptiness and a broken relationship with the Outside World of fact and reason and the inside world of Self. Those free of the obsessive belief that they are "better than a Negro" can recognize

* Winter of 1960–1961.
** May, 1961.

and name this trouble for what it is: but those caught in the sickness cannot see and dread to be shown.

I use the word *we* on many pages of this book: yet, never in this movement backward or forward has there been unity in the South. There have always been thousands of dissenters whose voices are muffled, whose acts are ignored. Always a few have continued to move forward even as the majority turned backward. But few of these have authority; and few can exert real leadership: their way is blocked. It is changing, yes; the few are steadily, slowly, becoming the many. But in the thirties and forties of which I now speak, it was mainly Franklin Roosevelt's personality that kept pulling us forward. I do not discount the handful of young preachers who risked their lives and their pulpits to bring insight and understanding, nor the occasional editor who spoke out boldly, nor the few college professors who never collaborated with white supremacy, nor the two or three lonely writers who stubbornly wrote what they felt they must write.

But these were the isolated few: unexpendable but not yet leaders.

At this time, there was a group of writers—poets, critics, novelists—who should have been on the side of change but were not. No writers in literary history have failed their region as completely as these did. They called themselves Fugitives; some preferred the name, Agrarians. They were not so opposed to change, if I read them accurately, as opposed to what we were *changing into*. With soft stinging denunciations, they took their stand against a future which they equated with the machine and industrial clatter; they felt the answer was to return to some sort of medieval pattern. They ignored evils of the Middle Ages and what is worse the cultural and political dynamics that made the period what it was. To them, the medieval was an ideal society and they wanted to go back to it.

Their books, their talk, their lectures were woven of the valid and the false: it is difficult to unbraid the strands. I am not sure it can be done. Let me say briefly this: The Fugitives recognized the evils of industrialized society; they saw clearly the increasing anonymity of men's activities, they recognized the overesteem of the scientific method. What they did not see was that men need not succumb to material values simply because the machine age has made them conspicuous, nor to a worship of science because it has become too powerful. Nor did they admit that the new technology and science could not be locked up in the dead brains of men who conceived them in the Eighteenth and Nineteenth centuries. They are *here*.

But instead of confronting these new realities the Fugitives turned away, after some eloquent denunciations, and sought the ancient "simplicities." In their search most of them ended up on northern university campuses.

They were so nearly right to be so wrong. And because their tones were cultured, even though their minds were not wholly so, they had great influence on the youngsters, sensitive, bright, who were their students: persuading many of them to refuse commitment to a future that was bound to be difficult, tangled, ambiguous but which must be created and should be created by the best minds and most sensitive spirits of our time. Instead, the Fugitives urged their students to busy themselves with literary dialectics, to support the "New Criticism" instead of a new life; and one way to do this was to search the pages of contemporary turgid writing for secret symbolic meanings where no meaning existed. The quickest way for a writer to be banned as an Outsider who did not belong to this little clique was for him to seek new words, new ways of interpreting the earth-shaking hour we live in.

The tone was southern but if one listened carefully

one could hear echoes of post-World War One German thinking. I do not think the Fugitives were a bit more lost in fogginess than is Heidegger * but they lacked the clarity of Jaspers' thinking, and the French Marcel, and the brilliance and humanity of Unamuno—and the later acrid wit of Sartre. And they had none of Kierkegaard's awesome honesty and blunt questioning which translations of his books at that time were revealing. They were searching the same paths: they just got lost too quickly.

The basic weakness of the Fugitives' stand, as I see it, lay in their failure to recognize the massive dehumanization which had resulted from slavery and its progeny, sharecropping and segregation, and the values that permitted these brutalities of spirit. They did not see that the dehumanization they feared the machine and science would bring was a *fait accompli* in their own agrarian region. They knew of the dual system of sharecropping and segregation, but something had blunted their imaginations for they had only a contactless association with it. By overlooking the gaping wounds and fissures of the present and the corruption of the spirit that had occurred in their region's past, they missed the major point in the Twentieth Century dialogue which has to do *not with systems* but with men's relationships. In a philosophical sense, they were a left-over from the Nineteenth Century.

But they were talented; and sensitive about minute matters; and warm about the uncontroversial: one cannot be angry with them, one only regrets that the South had to do without a brilliant, intellectual leadership that could face its ordeal and at the same time nourish its arid soul. These same Fugitives will argue that the role of artist does not embrace concern and action. They are wrong: →

---

* However, they had none of his searching intuition and philosophic subtlety.

Author's note. 1961.

a glance at the history of the European artist shows that the mainstream of art has always involved itself with the profound experiences of its age and man's commitment to them. An artist has to be that hard thing: a human being who is artist. What we value most in Camus, today, is what he has written, in compassionate concern, about his own and his people's moral turmoil.

As a writer, I, too, find it difficult to know when the human being in us should turn from the crises of our times and give way to the artist in us, when one can become totally absorbed in his painting or novel or poem. This absorption must occur; there must be withdrawal. When? How? There must also be a return to new commitments to human society. When? How?

Now back to this story of the changing South:

The New Deal gave the poor white so much, there was little room for resentment against the Negro, at first. Food in stomach, WPA jobs, money in the pocket, the NYA, rural electrification, and other projects gave to our people not understanding of human relations but a temporary tolerance as bland and undifferentiated as a well-fed, dry-diapered baby feels toward the world that surrounds it.

But when the war years came, 1941–1945, tolerance faded. There was more money than we had ever seen; higher wages, more jobs, better prices for crops. But there were also sharp deviations in our ways and vocabulary. Negroes in the Air Force were "flying over white heads." This made folks uneasy. "They were down in the field, now they're up in the sky." It shook the southern mind. And Negroes were murmuring, *If we fight for you, how about letting us vote?* Much of the unease was subliminal. But some of it came out in squawks and yapping. Southern Congressmen made shocking speeches spilling over with race hatred. There was a revival of the

Klan. And fresh panic about "intermarriage." Political candidates were once more dipping into cesspools for their speeches, and the once-poor and once-ignorant whites now climbing the first rungs of the status ladder were expressing an unformulated anxiety in outbursts of violence. It was obvious that prosperity does not automatically bring with it a commensurate esteem for human rights.

Yet, steadily, things were being done that needed to be done: we plunged into housing problems, we learned the mysteries of contour plowing and cover crops, our poor whites discovered what a sanitary unit is although some declared "no Federal governmint kin make us squat where we don't want to squat" and ruggedly kicked the damned thing over. But we were still going somewhere —though few would dare say what our destination would be. New roads were built—better fertilizer used—better seeds—new farm machinery. So it went. It was good occupational therapy, even though some cried to the heavens against the New Deal and the bossiness of the Federal government. The depression was easing and everybody knew it. Country folks who once sat on benches in front of the stores, wondering if they dared go in and ask for a little more credit having owed for groceries for a year or two, now jingled their dimes and quarters as they walked in and were as choosy as Doctor So-and-So's wife about what the butcher wrapped up for them. Storekeepers who were still opposed to the New Deal, paid their notes at the banks and the mortgage off their homes, bought a new sign with neon lights to put up in front of the store, and bragged about private initiative.

So things went. Our heart had not as yet given up its nub of greed and fear and hate and again and again these feelings shoved us down the wrong road. But even so, a few people were changing, a few were thinking, a few were loosening their grip on the past, not denying it existed but insisting that it not block off the years ahead.

Two steps forward . . . one step backward . . . three steps forward . . . two steps backward. Often it seemed, "This is where we came in ten years ago, or five, or three." There was no doubt that a new life had begun for our people: whether it was a good life was questionable, and just how many were affected we could not say. But one thing was certain: there was no solid South any more.

The old southern mold had cracked wide open and we had begun to see what it had done to us. This exposure was a tremendous experience: we actually saw ourselves for the first time; and seeing, we reached out and touched our arrogance, weighed the fear in hearts, peered in the chasms made by the separation of ideals from acts, slowly realized that anxiety, not love, dominated areas of our lives; began to see that things and machines and systems were our substitute for human relationships. We felt ourselves shrinking as we looked—and we could not endure the sight. Had we given ourselves time to get used to the newness, we might have seen that though we were not as tall as we had fantasied, we were tall enough for men. But we dared not look that far.

We saw instead—and this we could not admit—that the burden our fathers had believed to be the "colored race," was our own historical past, the weight on our spirits was that of our childhood, the change we felt unable to make was a change in ourselves. We were beginning to see how entwined are the white man's beliefs about sin and sex and segregation and money, and his mother, and his wife, and himself; how they loop over each other and send out roots into the mythic mind, then climb into the rational mind, making a jungle hard to find a way through.

Few in those days could endure this stark knowledge. And as anyone resists a touch on a raw nerve, so we

(South and North) resisted these new insights. We fought hard against understanding, we tried to live in a fog, we could not bear to see what was becoming clearer each day: that race relations are a part of the total human experience, not something history has set off in one corner of time.

We bargained with our future: we'll pay higher wages —if the government makes us; we'll leave off this one-crop system—if the government pays us enough to do so; we'll listen to words about soil erosion—if you don't talk about soul erosion; we'll even build some school-houses for the colored folks—if you pressure us hard enough; we'll do these things that will profit us financially and morally but we'll never admit Federal aid has helped one of us, we'll always call it "interference," and we won't give in about the sacred system of segregation. Never, never, never! If things change they've gotta change so slow we don't even notice it, otherwise—

And maybe it could have gone on this way, perhaps we could have blown history down a side road and kept it unmoving as our fantasies convinced us we could do, had not the atom bomb been dropped on Hiroshima on August 6, 1945. Maybe time would have been our ally had not that fatal day turned time into our mortal enemy. It was as though the whole world overnight had run up its clocks a hundred years. Walls fell. Barriers crumbled. Distances snapped together like elastic. Color, race, religion, nationality no longer had relevance. We were just people, two and a half billion frightened people, clinging to one small earth which could give us no pro-tection against the hate in men's heart and this dread power in their hand.

It was too big. Too much knowledge. Too sharp a break with the past. Too terrible a crime man had com-mitted against himself. We had been forced into a future that our feelings had no preparation for and our minds could grasp only crude approximations of. The scientists by their awesome success had shot us like a rocket into an unformed world.

And after a gasp, a shrill moment of terrified exclamation, we tried to deny. We slammed doors in our mind; we scratched August 6 off of the world calendar; we began to build wispy shaky bridges to tie us to a past that no longer was there. We began to throw up thin trembling walls that could no more shut out danger than a piece of paper can stop a fire but would serve only for a brief moment to shut out the sight of the future we were already in the center of.

People in panic moved toward their "own kind." Individuals clung to whatever securities of the past they could wrap around themselves. Mythic thinking superseded reason; the mob pushed the person off the streets of the world; new dictators took the place of old ones; Hitler was dead! Long live Stalin! Down slid the iron curtain cutting the Russian people away from the rest of us. Franklin Roosevelt had died—and now his words, *We have nothing to fear but fear itself*, were shattered by the bomb he had ordered built but would not, I think, have ordered dropped.

In the moral vacuum that followed it was inevitable that Joseph McCarthy (or someone like him) should arise as the "savior" of the American way; and, of course, he used as his storm troopers the anxieties which FDR had begged our people not to succumb to.

But McCarthy and his supporters, who so skillfully projected the people's fear upon "the Communists," could not have swayed millions had those millions not felt a confusion of guilt and dread they could not come to terms with. Who could fail to feel guilty when the whole earth was strewn with the symbols of man's broken faith with himself: concentration camps, firing squads,

Dachau, NKVD, burning crosses and the KKK, millions of starving children crying for food while we held in warehouses millions of tons of it which we did not give them because of technicalities of "world trade." Perhaps the deepest guilt came out of the unacknowledged fact that we Americans, as a people, were morally responsible for what had happened in Asia and yet, though responsible, we had known nothing about it. Our conscience became a bitter enemy as we tried to think and failed, tried to understand and failed, tried to make amends, knowing our deeds of mercy were almost too small to count. In despair many rejected their responsibility, saying, "The Others are to blame, not us."

Then the trials began: trials trials trials! It was as if everyone were compelled to make himself into a Grand Inquisitor and try the whole world for heresy. And the whole world would be found guilty—for we had betrayed the human spirit and we knew of all acts this is the most treasonable. No wonder men drove each other to take loyalty oaths and found everyone guilty of what they themselves had done.

Along with the madness and hysteria came what we call "reaction." Respectable people who dread violence and turmoil grew as afraid of good as of evil. Both seemed "extreme," both seemed equally disturbing to "peace and order." Honest but shortsighted people, even warmhearted people, became proud of their moral confusion, calling it "moderation." Those who cherished freedom and human rights and worked for them were put in the same moral category of "trouble makers" as the KKK and White Citizens Councils and the street mob. The self-termed "moderates" were those who spoke for law and order but would not speak against the segregation that threatened law and order; they would protest the lynching of men's bodies but not the lynching of their spirits; they opposed the mob on the street but not the mob in men's minds; they wanted laws obeyed but would not defend the moral values on which law is grounded. And as they grew in number, apathy became modish, silence a synonym for sanity, and complacency as much a sign of success and good breeding as an Ivy League suit.

In a curious way, southerner had become northern and northerner had become southern and both felt that everybody but themselves was slightly "unAmerican," especially if they seemed concerned about the human being who had become a world refugee, an Outsider, suspected and feared by politicians and officials everywhere.

2

The Chasm and the Bridge

THE YEARS go by. We are still fighting false battles or dead ones. We are still defending old worn-out systems, pitting them against each other. We know, our minds know, that the Twentieth Century dialogue has to do with relationships not systems; but we have not confessed it. Nor are we basing plans for the future on this knowledge. It is as if we cannot bridge the chasm between the past and what lies ahead. Perhaps we feel too insecure about the status of the human being. Man's spirit is certainly not held in high esteem, today: color is put above it by millions, and economic systems and nationalism and science and institutions by more millions, and gadgetry and profits by more and more millions.

And yet, we know the time is drawing near when we shall be compelled to take sides either for or against the continuing growth of the spirit of man. But most do not want to make a decision. It is this failure to make a fundamental choice that is driving us to take on more and more spurious conflicts while we cling to the old dead causes. How else can we explain the unreasonable way in which the European powers have clung to colonialism even though they know it is a corpse and know the consequences of this stubborn refusal to give up what is dead? How can they fail to measure the bitterness not only against them but against the entire West because they have failed to accept with wisdom and grace what is inevitable?

How else than by attributing it to a basic indecision can we explain the unloosening grip of "Marxism" and capitalism on each other, even though both have quietly died in the midst of the sound and fury? In Russia and the United States, private and public sectors of the economy are becoming more and more mixed as they bend to the exigencies of world conditions and their own country's internal needs—and this process is likely to continue. What, actually, are Russia and the United States fighting about? Do we know? Is it that we are promoting human freedom and they are promoting human welfare? I doubt that we should be willing to settle for that. We think, and rightly so, that we are deeply concerned for the people's welfare. But—and here things tangle—though we declare to the world our unshakeable belief in freedom our defense of it at home has been faltering and our failure, even now, to give the Negro group its full rights has shaken the world's faith in our words. But Russia, too, has failed in lamentable ways: not only by its refusal to let its citizens speak freely and choose their leaders freely, but in its loudly advertised plan for the common people's welfare; it certainly has not made good its promises. So where are we? What is it all about? Can it be true, as some neutrals say, that Russia looks toward the future and we look toward the past? Is the fight about what age we are living in? Or is it as others say, that Russia is for the peasants of the world and we are for the middle classes? Would we settle for that? Or is it as cynics say, that the whole mess is a raw struggle for power? Whatever the answer, the issues are insanely confused.

The same confusion hovers over the question of racism here at home: we know White Supremacy is indefensible in today's world, we know that as an idea it is dead, but the bitter struggle goes on, South and North: wasting minds and time and hearts and economic resources, tying us to a past where ghost battles ghost. And while this happens the human spirit sits on the rim of things, waiting.

Why does this have to be?

I do not know the full answer, of course. I think it is, partly, because we have lost a vision of man. We are not sure how different he actually is from animal or vegetable or rock or machine. It is partly, I think, because we have ceased trying to relate ourselves to God: we no longer even cry that God is dead; instead, we have named him an hypothesis, a dream, and turned him over to the laboratory to "prove." And since we have stopped searching for God we have stopped searching for ultimate meaning, saying there is no purpose in human existence. Hence all is absurdity, all is nothing. The more honest among those who want God "proved" tend to seek uneasy solace in neo-nihilism; or, putting heart above logic, in humanism,—while the less honest settle for their own brand of idol worship, sacrificing all to success or skin color or capitalism or communism or their work or their pleasure, whispering, *Let's don't think about it.*

But whether we think or don't think, the soul is left free-floating and becomes lost and we grow more and more lonely, and are filled with *angst.* We begin to deny our essence; we do not see that the human situation is conditioned on uncertainty and based on fragmentation, that its inner laws force upon it splits and fissures and uncounted separations which we must bridge in order to find wholeness. But we cannot admit this, and turn away: trying not to believe the bridging is a necessity, and that sometimes, faith is the only bridge available. We still want to believe man is, by nature, solid and proof-sure.

We forget Eden. We forget that it was man's tearing himself in two that made him human; that the Primal Moment for him was when he stepped back and looked at himself. Awareness—call it Eve, if you like—came between him and his Self. And out of this awareness came the symbol and the word, and love, and wonder and curiosity and hope and hate and greed and the dream and the painful, hurting knowledge that he is a torn thing always in need of being tied to something else.

But modern man is embarrassed about this need to be related; he keeps wishing he were solid and self-sufficient and tries to behave as if he is. And holding on to this false confidence, and refusing faith, he cuts himself off from what he need not do without—almost as if to convince himself that he can do so. Being armored in arrogance he finds it hard to genuflect to an unproved God, and impossible to relate to Him. How strange! For we all cling to meanings we cannot prove just as we cling to love and hope, and to art whose importance to the human being in us, though unproved, we are somehow sure of.

Every intelligent person knows, today, that proof is a valid requirement on some levels of experience and totally irrelevant on others. But there is a difference between knowing and accepting of what one knows. Around this theme of "proof" we have piled confusions which have intensified anxiety until some of us are unable to relate to anything. Instead, we try to find a system to fuse ourselves with, or we spin out ideologies and chain ourselves to them.

There are many other causes of anxiety, of course: beginning with what happens in our hearts when we are young and extending into the world in every direction. But perhaps the most obvious is our dread of annihilation from bombs which are increasing in power and number.

This strange whizzing business of nuclear armaments, the rockets and the missiles and the rest of it, shakes us to our depths. And added to this, is the bleak certainty that too much power rests in too few hands and some of these hands belong to underlings who may—it is possible —in a sudden dark moment, push the wrong button.

These matters press hard on us. Where do we turn for the strength simply to endure?

But there is another way to look at the human situation; a way that may give us new purpose and hope. The crisis in human affairs which we feel occurring on many levels and which seems, often, to be intensifying as it spreads is basically caused by the slow-growing realization that from here on out we have our destiny in our own hands; and this destiny is not so much concerned with where we are going as with what we are becoming.

It is as if God has brought the Earth people through a long, labored journey of slow growth and evolvement beginning four billion years ago and now has put everything into their hands—even their relationship with Him. How it started, we don't know. Some say a little cloud of neutrons may have appeared in the emptiness, and in three or four minutes things as we think of them today—neutrons and protons and electrons—may have begun the fabulous and unending binding and dispersal out of which the universe has come. Now, after a billion years of life's natural evolution—during which living forms succeeded and replaced living forms again and again until finally a creature was made who could stand off and look at himself and speak—God, in effect, is saying to Man:

From now on, you do it; use your own culture, the knowledge you have accumulated, your own ideas and dreams, your own skills and technics and inventiveness–and become what you like. As a human being, you are only partially evolved; if you want to, you can continue changing yourself. But it is up to you. There are laws you cannot break, even though you try: you cannot return to a one-cell existence; you cannot become any of the forms of life I created before you—jellyfish, or animal or even neolithic man; you cannot reverse the irreversible. You have your natural inheritance and it is within you but from now on you are man, cultured by man; not nature's doing. Call yourself modern, if you like, but you cannot stand still because you are not nearly completed. You are now in a dangerous state of flux: you could with ease become a monster or destroy yourself and your earth, but you cannot move backward. You are only a broken piece of life, remember, and cannot live without The Others. To live as a man you must somehow find ways to relate to Me, to yourself, to other men, to knowledge and to uncertainty, to past and future, all you have made: your art, your science, your things, your understanding; and you must somehow learn to bridge your mythic to your rational mind, you must somehow learn the difference in merging and relating. This is a big part of your trouble, your forgetting this elementary lesson. In all your history you have not really learned it. But when you do, your addiction to proofs will lessen and you will realize that you are a strange, versatile and fascinating creature who can live on many levels simultaneously and in many communities of thought whose laws are different—such as science and art and religion; in only one of these is proof needed, in the others, it is irrelevant; your trouble comes, it always has, when you try to merge them into one instead of relating them to each other and to yourself, permitting each to abide by its inner laws which I, God, have made and which you, Man, cannot break. You can never become one with what you love or hate or fear or long for: only related; therefore your loneliness will always, like your shadow, be with you.

There must be millions of people across the earth listening to an inner voice which is whispering words similar to these. At least, I like to think so.

When we consider man's evolution which is now in his own hands, when we ponder the awesome possibilities for good and evil that he controls, we see the task before

him as prodigious. But it is also magnificent adventure.
Yet it could come to a quick and terrible end. Imaginations cringe as they peer into this dark uncertainty. But
one cannot think about it long without feeling new
purpose stir the heart; a thin edge of meaning touches
the mind—and suddenly one believes, again. Believes
what? Let me say it this way: I believe every creative
act, every poem, every painting, every honest question
or honest dissent, every gesture of courage and faith and
mercy and concern will count; every new awareness will
count; every time we defend the human spirit it will
count; every time we turn away from arrogance and
lies, this, to, will count in the project called *Human
Being Evolving*. And as we think of what could happen
to the human race, if we want it to happen—when we
think of the billions of dormant seeds in our nature and
culture awaiting warmth and cultivation, we find ourselves ready to pick up our little watering pot and sacks
of rich soil and start out on the million-year plan for
the growing of a New Man. We may in our thinking
need to stretch the old-fashioned minute into a year;
and the year into a thousand years, as we map our way.
No matter: time can be nothing or something, long or
short, here or not here; human beings learned, long ago,
a few tricks in dealing with it. We shall soon be able to
cup a thousand years in the mind quite comfortably.

Against the sounding board of this gigantic purpose
to which we can commit ourselves if we want to, the
sniveling we have heard in recent years makes an un-
endurable sound. We grow angry at those who deliberately try to shrivel the person into something mean
and weak. They become the earth's enemy—not to be
killed but to be deaf to. Set against this plan of evolution
we see the battles now being fought, cold and hot—and
the armaments that make them possible—as something
crazy and useless and wasteful. Who cares, we begin to

say, about either capitalism or communism! They are mere epicycles that have had their day. Who cares about skin color when he discovers a human being inside himself or his neighbor! Who cares about national power when power belongs in this century to all or to none! What we need to do is get on with the job; on with the art and the science and the philosophy and the technology of evolution which will be slow—we are not forgetting this—but not as slow as in the past. We have found ways to compress time; and we have so much access to energy that some, in their panic, want to reject all of it because it seems to be without limit. But we also have the inner strength to match the new powers; and I hope we have the wisdom to protect us from the men who would exploit them in their mad confusion.

It is possible that the Devil is luring us into outer space to divert us from this project of evolving a new being. But perhaps we are capable of both giant tasks. To try either of them without tapping our moral and psychic resources, and without safeguarding the soul in us would be an irreversible mistake.

So we stand: as in every crisis since life began, confronting both good and evil in our nature and in our world. The only difference is that the good and the evil now have unlimited potentialities and the size of our world is expanding every day. But so is the size of our imagination and our love. Geography is no longer a deterrent to relating our concern and hope or hate or fears to others, however distant they may be.

Our home is the whole earth but home is also the place we were born. Let us return for another look at the South:

So little, in comparison with the vast changes sweeping the world, has happened in our region during the past decade. We have grown more prosperous, we have more things and we produce more things; we have better communication with the rest of our country and with each other; our population has shifted from rural to urban centers, great migrations of blacks and whites to the North are still in progress and hence the center of racial conflict is shifting, or rather breaking into a number of small centers from which trouble radiates. But we are still fixed on old fears; our demagogues at home and in Congress are still wailing about mixing and mongrelizing and "our way of life" and the "outsiders" and the "agitators"; and are still giving communism credit for every brave, intelligent, decent act done by a southerner.

But events are loosening our grip on the past: Supreme Court decisions and new implementation of Civil Rights bills have crumbled segregation in the Armed Services and are in process of doing so in employment in governmental agencies and industries which hold government contracts; public schools are slowly, reluctantly, obeying these decisions; other decisions affecting interstate travel and bus and railroad stations and airports are opening these, without segregation, to all our citizens, although here, too, the local opposition is fierce and irrational; numerous secondary court decisions and Presidential directives are pushing us forward even though the people still struggle wildly and bitterly.

Added to these firm pressures are the "incidents" which release a horde of ghosts who wander inside and outside us, terrorizing our best and worst citizens, each in a different way. For these happenings, these communal acts, are loaded with symbolism and behave like explosives: throwing the stuff within our minds into the open where all can see. We dread this sharp, savage exposure, the spill-out of hate and obscenity and stupidity. And perhaps, most of all, we dread to confront the emptiness that is revealed at the center of our peoples' lives.

The mob has become, for us, not only an ugly reality where people may get hurt, it has also become a new symbol of our spiritual deprivation and moral chaos. There are worse things than mobs: segregation is worse, and the continuous drip drip of shame and indignity that goes along with it is worse, and the refusal to come clean and confess our wrong-doing, and the reluctance to commit ourselves to the future. All this is worse and far more threatening to our survival than is a mob. But to many white southerners, today, a mob has become our most feared ghost, possessing a numinous power that shakes us to our depths. All the good elements of a community—and some of the evil—can be counted on to take their stand against the mob on the street; certainly, after experiencing one. Only the lunatic fringe and the criminal element seem not to feel its symbolic significance. But their leaders do. These men know the community's fear of a mob and deliberately use the threat of stirring up one to keep the good people silent and passive. "You see what happens?" they say; and the good people sometimes agree that all would have been fine had only the "agitators" and the "outsiders" and the "communist elements" stayed away, and left it to them, although most of them had, up to that moment, done exactly nothing to change the racial *status quo*.

The dread comes, of course, from the naked exposure that occurs. Actually, the community often improves after this Return of the Repressed takes place. Good things begin to happen, not immediately, but soon; public opinion becomes more informed; the people's apathy lessens, their complacency shows a few fissures; and reason, at least to a limited degree, prevails. Little Rock greatly harmed American prestige and our foreign relations are still suffering from its effect on world opinion. But Little Rock, itself, is better off than it was before its débâcle. A perverted kind of catharsis, yes; but catharsis seems to have occurred. New Orleans harmed American prestige and worsened the injury to our foreign relations which Little Rock inflicted, but New Orleans, too, will "come to its senses," and the process of change will be quickened.

The Emmitt Till case . . . Clinton . . . Birmingham . . . Montgomery . . . Anniston . . . Americus . . . the riot on the campus of the University of Georgia . . . Jackson, Mississippi—and more and more and still more incidents have shaken the heart and mind of American people. They have lessened apathy and complacency, and have stirred consciences wherever consciences can be stirred by acts of cruelty and arrogance. But this business of burning down the village in order to roast the pig is expensive in its waste of the human spirit, in its muddling of minds, in its loss to the community of new industry, and civic order and that tranquillity which is necessary for creativity. But it will go on until we change our leaders to those who know and can use the magic of the good word; who understand the difference in facts and symbols and who can keep from merging their mythic with their rational mind. Heart is needed, too; concern, compassion, a sense of what it is going to take to survive in an uncreated future. But even though people have these good feelings and desires, if they cannot handle their symbols, if they cannot keep the mythic mind out of the rational mind's business, there is inevitable trouble.

Here is the place where we in the South are having difficulty. (Is it necessary to add that others throughout the world are having the same kind of trouble?) For our people mingle symbols and facts as if they were molasses and feathers. When we were children, our nurse, to keep us quiet, often poured molasses in our hands and then gave us a wad of feathers—which resulted in our being preoccupied for hours. Any child, having had this experience, knows there is no such thing as picking the feathers from either hand: the only device that works is soap and water. But in racial affairs, and others, too, we have not learned this: and the old molasses-and-feathers game goes on and on and on and on, supervised by politicians who always have more of the same if the constituents grow restless.

We cannot get along without symbols, it would be unthinkable. But they are full of strange power and can destroy us quickly when used improperly—as the Germans' experience with them demonstrated. They need to be handled as carefully as nuclear energy and the rules for doing so should be learned by all. Symbols should be kept in their place; they should not be mixed with facts and then treated as though they are facts; nor should facts be mixed with symbols and treated as though they are symbols, for facts have their place, too. It is the merging and mixing that causes most of the trouble. The trouble is worsened when "ordinary acting" is suddenly, without warning, transformed into symbolic acting. We feel turned upside down when this happens; much as we should feel were we to see a painting walk down Main Street arm in arm with the village banker. In such a situation we are likely to decide that we are no longer in a reasonable, factual world but have been transported to the mythic world where art and fairy tales and poetry live—or else that we might as well face the dreary fact that things are out of order in our own heads.

But this mixing of the levels of thinking, this confusion of the qualities of reality has been accepted by many in Dixie as a normal way to behave. This is revealed in our attitude toward the word, *relationships*. On the rational level of the mind we understand that a relationship is a kind of bridge, a dialogue, a question and answer. When we use the word, we see in our mind one person relating or responding to another, etc. But the mythic mind sees nothing of the kind: it sees mongrelization, fusing, merging, melting. Why? Because the mythic mind is not capable of relating: its *modus operandi* is one of spreading: it is not restrained by barriers of time and space, or cause and effect, or facts that contradict, or logical categories. It licks like a flame at everything that comes near it, making its own kind of Phoenix out of the ashes. It likes to create something big out of the small: it can take one quality, such as whiteness and cover a neighborhood or a quarter of the earth with it, declaring that all beneath this great white sheet are the "same."

Once tangled in the stuff of the mythic mind, it is difficult to escape, unless you are an artist. Thousands of fairly intelligent people get permanently stuck in such feathers and molasses as "The Outsiders did it," . . . "Leave us alone and we'll take care of things" . . . "We white folks and black folks were getting along just fine until the agitators came" . . . "It is the extremists on both sides who cause the trouble." The rational mind would be embarrassed by this business; it would keep trying to fit the statements to facts: the facts of a changing world, the facts of local conditions, the facts of African nationalism, the facts of the American Constitution. But the mythic mind couldn't care less. Why should its statements fit facts? There is no law in the mythic region to make them do so.

It is, however, as dangerous to overvalue facts and undervalue symbols as it is to mix them.

We have brought much trouble upon ourselves in Asia and Africa because we have turned away when we thought what we heard was not sensible or not based on "realistic facts." The colonies have been demanding for a long time that they be given their freedom; and finally, reluctantly, the powers are now turning the countries back to their rightful owners. Listening to their demands for freedom, we Americans have tended to think that the new nations, after experiencing political domination, now want a form of government that will be democratic, that will give the citizens full voice and control over their political affairs, and that will safeguard their civil liberties. Actually, nothing is further from the truth. What they want, these Asians and Africans, is to be free of the old symbols of contempt that they were burdened with by their colonial masters. They have not forgotten, they cannot forget, that as the symbols of contempt were being laid on them their old symbols, which had given them a sense of dignity and value, were being stripped away. These new nations are, in a sense, without symbols, today, and men cannot live that way. To them, democracy is merely a fine idea. Whatever symbolic meaning it may have for Americans, for the former colonial people it has little—and this little (tied to the fact that the colonial powers also called themselves 'democracies') carries with it some bad memories. *Democracy*, certainly at present, cannot meet their need for symbols. But *equality* does. And they will trample the earth to get it. They may cry freedom as they trample but in their hearts they are singing of equality.

All men are equal is a phrase heavy with meaning, powerful in its emotional effect upon those who have been long oppressed by the white man. But what are the facts about this statement? Are men equal? No. They are not equal, will never be, have never been. Indeed, the end of the human race would have come long ago, had they been equal, or the same. We are different in ten thousand ways from each other and we know it. We know, too, that out of these differences, these infinite variations, big and small, comes mankind's chance of evolving into a new being. We also know that "equal" while relevant when we speak of refrigerators is senseless when we speak of people. And the Asian and African leaders know it, too. But they also know that underneath the surface facts of men's differences, the symbolic truth is that we *are equal as human beings:* equal before God; equal in that we are born and will die; equal in that we get sick, get well, grow, and learn and become aware and are hurt and can be reasoned with; equal in that we can burn with anger and light up with hope and can work and create and destroy and sleep and dream and make love and kill and use words and symbols, and ask questions; equal in that we long to reach out toward the great Unknown; equal, too, in our need of each other, for the weak need the strong and the strong cannot long survive without the weak.

All this is true. But there are "realistic" facts in the Asian-African situation that we Americans keep feeling sensible men should put first: food, for instance, when people are starving; medicines when half the population is ill; housing when so many are without shelter; and schooling and hospitals and roads and better farming and electric power, and so on. We may be right. It might be more sensible to nourish the body before bothering much about the soul and the heart, but it would be difficult to persuade people that this is so. Symbol-hunger is importunate, it pushes sensible needs and facts away from it. We southerners should remember this from our own experience. Whether we understand or not, the African and Asian leaders do; and though they are working to meet their people's physical necessities, what they long for, dream about and connive to get is "equality"— equality as persons, equality in terms of human rights, equality in the United Nations—and let's say it, "racial equality." They want a black face to count as much as a white face does in every situation in the world. And what they hate and fear more than hunger and more than death are those symbols: segregation, apartheid, colonialism—and the actions that are tied fast to them. Of course they know the facts of the communist threat to their newly found political freedom; but remember, these are *facts:* they do not enter the part of the mind where the old symbols crouch breathing out poison.

When African leaders tell us they are not interested in communism or capitalism, we should listen. If we don't, once more the white man's blindness, his own confusion about facts and symbols may drive these leaders to pick out of the historic mud a symbol on which they *can* nourish their hurt dignity: Black Supremacy. It has happened before, in our own South. After the Civil War, when things were in chaos and misery was everywhere and people were without food and learning and shelter and medicine, our politicians picked up the symbol of White Supremacy and made it a flag and a doctrine and a passion by which to "unify" poor white and rich white (who felt they had little in common) in a mutual hostility against the Negro. It was one easy way to build power. In Africa, there are tribal hostilities hard to deal with, prickly and mind-consuming which pull against national loyalties and aims. Why not siphon off the tribal fury and turn it into hatred of whites who continue so stubbornly to think of themselves as superior? A black leader would be stupid not to be tempted—and a tragic fool, were he to succumb to the temptation.

For the South, for Africa, for the whole world, the road to the future is piled high with such psychological and political impedimenta. Some of it is junk and waste; some of it is pulsating with energy. And in addition to these blocks, there are the floods of emotion which blind men to their direction—brought on by frustration and physical exhaustion and verbal confusion as well as by sheer poverty.

But not all people are blind: more and more see what it is all about. In every country this is so. In the South— and once more, let's turn back to it—our big hope lies in the fact that ten years ago, only a few saw things clearly; now, thousands see. Not only the lonely individuals and the Cassandras, but groups—and these groups are growing larger and more energetic. We have the churchwomen who have patiently been untangling the racial confusion for years; the Southern Regional Council; the Human Relations Councils; civic clubs, the League of Women Voters, the Ministerial Councils, and more and more newspaper reporters and editors; some still see as if through a glass darkly, but they, at least, keep peering. And there are a few writers and artists who understand the ambivalent hungers beneath these seething tensions. But the hopeful sign is that just plain people, men and women, rich and poor, are searching for the right questions. In addition, there are the groups of parents who intuitively avoid mythic matters, edging away from radioactive symbols, holding tight to reason, as they stress "keeping our schools open so children may become educated." This simple statement is so sane, so sensible that defenses have fallen before it as though Joshua had once more picked up his trumpet.

And the Negro? For so long, the Negro in the South was silent. There were many exceptions, but there appeared to be some validity in the old demagogues' statements that "the niggers like it this way." Of course, they never liked it but they acquiesced in the condition imposed upon them because they felt it had to be. Like peasants the world over, the southern Negro was too impoverished and illiterate for a long time to find a way out of his dilemma. So he settled for another life in heaven; and planned for it—and his hope and faith kept him sane and shrewd as he whittled out defenses against the hard and the hateful of this earth. That the Negro has been a worthy antagonist, any white man who has lived near him will admit; for there is no white man who has not at one time or another been worsted in a deal with a Negro. He learned to outcheat the cheaters and sometimes delighted in his amoral bargaining. Nevertheless, he had lost his human birthright and he knew it. And it has always showed: in his laughing talk and his weeping song—or as he danced off his rage. He has, through the years, repelled anxiety by the sheer power of his endurance and by a persisting vitality. However the white man may have enslaved the Negro's body he did not enslave his soma—his inner stamina, his functions were kept free; and this audacious fact is one of the causes of some white men's envy and fury.

Now things have changed. The change has been abrupt and dramatic and has pierced the depths of the southern situation. There is, today, a revolution going on within the Negro's mind. He is discovering his powers: moral, economic, psychological, political.

It startled him when he realized that big department stores are dependent upon his dollars; he was slow to learn that his own group spends billions and can shake the southern economy; that often his trade is the difference between profit and loss; that his vote counts; that his voice has moral weight in the world's councils; that his talents are cherished by everybody; and that the winds of change are blowing him in the right direction.

Realizing his strength, he has begun to resist the old segregated way of life. Resistance did not spring out of nothing; for decades, a few Negroes and whites had been preparing the way, and events in Asia and Africa had stirred imaginations. Let us say, it seemed to begin suddenly a few years ago: when the young Martin Luther King led the Montgomery Negroes in their passive resistance to segregated local buses. Their famous walking to work stirred the world as nothing had since Gandhi's walk to the sea to make salt in protest against the British salt tax. The walking continued for more than a year and during that time Negroes opened their eyes and ears and began to listen to their own cries for help.

Once begun, it could not stop. More and more protests —and more. But the voices were quiet, conciliating, firm; and there was no violence on the part of leaders and almost none among their followers. Their self-discipline, their compassion, their knowledge of the redemptive power of suffering amazed the entire world.

In February of 1960, came the first of the young Negro students with their dramatic and nonviolent sit-ins at segregated lunch counters—in protest against the old system. And then, in May, 1961, Freedom Rides started. Their aim was to test the treatment given Negroes in interstate travel in the South. The white mobs gathered and a bus was burned and wholesale jailings of "the agitators"—the nonviolent group—took place in Alabama and Mississippi, even though Robert Kennedy, the U. S. Attorney General, did all in his power to protect the "Riders." And through it all, the Freedom Riders retained their calm and used no violence to counter violence; and the Negroes' determination throughout the South—and the nation—hardened. They will not stop now until they arrive at their destination, which is the achievement of full civil rights as American citizens.

The philosophy of these students is a mixture of Thoreau, Jefferson, Gandhi, Martin Buber, the teachings of Jesus and something uniquely theirs: humor, and a natural sense of historical direction.

They are greatly influenced, and frequently advised, by Martin Luther King—a personable, intelligent, and deeply religious young man with nerves of iron and emotions that lie down like lambs within him. He holds stubbornly to his values, is not easily tempted, and will, I think, never succumb to rage against the white man; he is for the human being and has taken his stand.

The nation-wide enemies of the group of nonviolent resisters were too startled at first to organize against them. But a virulent campaign is now on, worthy of Joseph McCarthy, to throw heavy suspicion on their loyalty and motives and affiliations. Even so, the majority of Americans are sympathetic and the leaders in our government are, although many find it difficult to accept the philosophy of nonviolence which these students sustain themselves on.

So it goes: violence and nonviolence; factual arguments and gobbledygook; quiet protest and noisy mob. Terrorism flares up in one town while the neighboring town is developing a courageous concern; sudden insights light up public opinion, foul words blur the situation, one act of heroism stirs the heart, one cruel incident pierces the conscience—then apathy creeps back, until another incident occurs.

If only we could afford this zigzagging walk into the future! But each day the slowness becomes more dangerous. What will quicken us? What will illumine our minds? What can be said or done that will compel us to slough off inertia and complacency and take our stand for the human being against his unnumbered enemies? If only we could see the brokenness in each of us and the necessity for relationships; if we could realize our talent for bridging chasms that have always been and always will be. If only we could rise up against the killers of man's dream. But, sometimes, that killer of dreams is in us and we do not know how to rid ourselves of it.

Once, long ago, a little crazy hypothesis was thrown across a dark sky and left there. And people could never forget it. Religions were built by its light, poets' minds shone in its brightness, political systems used its warmth to draw men closer together, and science examined it cautiously and "proved" it to be the essence of sanity, the seed of human growth. It may be only a bedtime story that men told themselves in their loneliness; it may be a lie: this sanctity of the human being, this importance of man the individual, this right of the child to grow, but when it is proved so, there will no longer be an earth to witness the lie's triumph and no men here to mourn the loss of their dream.

So we stand: tied to the past and clutching at the stars! Only by an agonizing pull of our dream can we wrench ourselves from such fixating stuff and climb into the unknown. But we have always done it and we can do it again. We have the means, the technics, we have the knowledge and insight and courage. All have synchronized for the first time in history. Do we have the desire? That is a question that each of us must answer for himself.

And now, I must break off this story that has not ended; a story that is, after all, only one small fragment, hardly more than a page in a big book where is being recorded what happened to men and women and children of the earth during the Great Ordeal when finally they separated themselves a little way from nature and assumed the burden of their own evolution.